Summary of Contents

JUMP START FOUNDATION

BY SYED FAZLE RAHMAN
& JOE HEWITSON

Jump Start Foundation

by Syed Fazle Rahman and Joe Hewitson

Product Manager: Simon Mackie
English Editor: Kelly Steele
Technical Reviewer: Ryan Reese
Cover Designer: Alex Walker

Notice of Rights

Notice of Liability

Trademark Notice

Published by SitePoint Pty. Ltd.

48 Cambridge Street Collingwood
VIC Australia 3066
Web: www.sitepoint.com
Email: business@sitepoint.com

ISBN 978-0-9924612-7-0 (print)

ISBN 978-0-9943469-0-2 (ebook)
Printed and bound in the United States of America

About Syed Fazle Rahman

Syed Fazle Rahman is a passionate web developer and technical writer from India. He is the co-founder of devmag.io, a community for software developers to hang out and talk about programming. Syed is also the author of the book Jump Start Bootstrap[1], published by SitePoint. When not programming, Syed can be found reading books and playing games.

About Joe Hewitson

Growing up with a love for coding, Joe delights in staying on the cutting edge of software development, especially web technology. This has led him to professional success ranging from the creation of web based, healthcare applications to dynamic CMS frameworks. He spends much of his free time exploring new web technologies and sharing the knowledge he's gained with those kind enough to listen.

About SitePoint

SitePoint specializes in publishing fun, practical, and easy-to-understand content for web professionals. Visit http://www.sitepoint.com/ to access our blogs, books, newsletters, articles, and community forums. You'll find a stack of information on JavaScript, PHP, Ruby, mobile development, design, and more.

[1] http://www.sitepoint.com/store/jump-start-bootstrap/

To my lovely parents, troublesome brother, cute sister, and my best buddy, Sandeep.

—Syed

To all those still hungry for knowledge, may this book only whet your appetite.

—Joe

Table of Contents

Preface

Crafting a modern, professional website from scratch takes a lot of time and effort. Sites today need to be responsive, mobile first, slickly designed, and fast. That's where Zurb's Foundation framework can help you. It provides a vast array of HTML components and a grid system that makes creating professional, responsive templates a snap, significantly cutting down development time.

Frameworks such as Foundation are useful for everyone, but are a blessing for novice developers. All the intricate CSS and JavaScript required to create complex web components are prewritten. Only some HTML markup is needed to make them work. More experienced developers can customize the framework with Sass.

Throughout this book, our aim is to provide a complete guide to the Foundation framework. We'll cover how we can build beautiful responsive websites without needing to gain expertise in advanced web development techniques. We'll also discuss the various useful components that Foundation provides out of the box, and explore ways of customizing the look and feel of Foundation to generate completely unique designs.

Who Should Read This Book

This book is suitable for beginner- to intermediate-level web designers and developers. Experience of HTML and CSS is assumed, while some knowledge of JavaScript is helpful.

Conventions Used

You'll notice that we've used certain typographic and layout styles throughout this book to signify different types of information. Look out for the following items.

Code Samples

Code in this book will be displayed using a fixed-width font, like so:

```
<h1>A Perfect Summer's Day</h1>
<p>It was a lovely day for a walk in the park. The birds
were singing and the kids were all back at school.</p>
```

If the code is to be found in the book's code archive, the name of the file will appear at the top of the program listing, like this:

example.css

```
.footer {
  background-color: #CCC;
  border-top: 1px solid #333;
}
```

If only part of the file is displayed, this is indicated by the word *excerpt*:

example.css *(excerpt)*

```
  border-top: 1px solid #333;
```

If additional code is to be inserted into an existing example, the new code will be displayed in bold:

```
function animate() {
  new_variable = "Hello";
}
```

Where existing code is required for context, rather than repeat all of it, ⋮ will be displayed:

```
function animate() {
  ⋮
  return new_variable;
}
```

Some lines of code should be entered on one line, but we've had to wrap them because of page constraints. A ➥ indicates a line break that exists for formatting purposes only, and should be ignored:

```
URL.open("http://www.sitepoint.com/responsive-web-design-real-user-
➥testing/?responsive1");
```

Tips, Notes, and Warnings

Hey, You!

Tips will give you helpful little pointers.

Ahem, Excuse Me ...

Notes are useful asides that are related—but not critical—to the topic at hand. Think of them as extra tidbits of information.

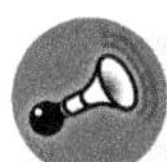

Make Sure You Always ...

... pay attention to these important points.

Watch Out!

Warnings will highlight any gotchas that are likely to trip you up along the way.

Supplementary Materials

http://www.sitepoint.com/store/jump-start-foundation/
: The book's website, containing links, updates, resources, and more.

https://github.com/spbooks/jsfoundation1
: The downloadable code archive for this book.

http://community.sitepoint.com/c/html-css
: SitePoint's forums, for help on any tricky web problems.

`books@sitepoint.com`
: Our email address, should you need to contact us for support, to report a problem, or for any other reason.

Want to take your learning further?

Thanks for choosing to buy a SitePoint book. Would you like to continue learning? You can now gain unlimited access to ALL SitePoint books and courses, plus high-quality books from our selected partners, at SitePoint Premium[1]. Enroll now and start learning today!

[1] https://www.sitepoint.com/premium/home

Chapter 1

Building a Foundation

Ready to get your hands dirty with all that the Zurb Foundation framework has to offer? Such enthusiasm is certainly commendable, and if you're as excited about CSS frameworks as I am, jumping in headfirst is likely why you're here in the first place. Diving right in is exactly what we'll do ... in a moment. Before we get too far ahead of ourselves, let's take a second to get our bearings and make sure we have a firm grasp on the ideas and concepts behind the Foundation framework.

As you read through the sections of this chapter, you'll gain a solid understanding of what the Foundation framework is and how it can be of benefit to your web projects. You'll find this genuinely useful information presented in three sections. The first will cover foundational aspects of CSS frameworks in a general sense. What they are, why they're useful, and some important concepts. In the second section you'll find a high-level overview describing the CSS framework for which this book was written. It's here that you'll discover the main intricacies that set the Zurb Foundation framework apart from its peers. Finally, the third section will have you roll up your sleeves and begin your *Jump Start Foundation* journey by setting up a basic project with Zurb's CSS framework.

Ready to dive in? Let's get started!

Introduction to CSS Frameworks

If you've never used a software **framework** before, it might be beneficial to think of it in the construction sense. When building a house, one of the first steps of actual construction is the development of the frame. Built out of any number of basic elements, it serves as a unified structure supporting the rest of the house. Without it, you'd have nothing to hinge your doors on or place your walls against. Similarly, a CSS framework provides a styling structure from which you can more easily build your web projects.

I know this all sounds well and good for a general contractor, but how can it help you build a better web project? CSS frameworks grant you the ability to develop web projects quickly using predeveloped CSS components. There's no need to reinvent the wheel every time you start a new project. To use most of these components, you simply write down the required HTML markup and you're done. It makes it easier to create a basic web user interface prototype without having to write down many CSS or JavaScript codes.

I'll give you a quick example of how CSS frameworks work in practice. When creating a new web project without the aid of a CSS framework, until stylesheets are created to define even the simplest of elements, your resulting pages will look little better than if they were created with a typewriter. When the time comes to begin styling, every facet of the page structure must be considered and styled appropriately—everything from the most basic paragraphs to fully customized div containers. Not only do these basic styles need to be developed from scratch, but also more advanced components such as image galleries or JavaScript features must likewise be manually developed or integrated into the project.

You can imagine (if you've spent any appreciable amount of time developing web projects from scratch) how this process can quickly become time consuming. But with a CSS framework, this process is made drastically easier by using many of its built-in CSS and JavaScript components.

Instead of tediously defining each basic element of a new web project, you only need to worry about styles you'd like to customize further. This can cut large amounts of hand-styling out of the web development equation, letting you focus more on refining the look of your project rather than defining every piece of its appearance.

Furthermore, it reduces countless hours tinkering with fussy JavaScript with the hope of adding fancy effects. For example, adding a simple thumbnail feature to your project would likely require dozens of lines of code without having use of prebuilt libraries. Heck, even with jQuery you'd need to include the requisite scripts, set up an anchor with a call to the action, and finally style the thumbnail itself.

With a CSS framework such as Foundation, it's as simple as this:

```
<a class="th" href="../img/image.png">
    <img src="../img/image.png">
</a>
```

By simply specifying the thumbnail class, `th` in the case of Foundation, the image is automatically styled and the required JavaScript applied to create a polished thumbnail image. Again, this is just one example of how CSS frameworks can make your life easier as a web developer. We'll be learning more about Foundation components and how it is easy it is to employ them in our websites from Chapter 4 onwards; however, to check out the complete list of components and their usages, you can always refer to the Foundation documentation.[1]

Becoming Acquainted with Foundation

The Foundation framework began as a humble style guide used by the folk at Zurb,[2] a product design company, back in 2008 for all their client projects. It wasn't long before they realized that their development methods were much too slow and inefficient. What they needed was a library of frequently used tools that they could re-implement in a quick and easy fashion. Sounds like a CSS framework, doesn't it? That's exactly what they built, and presumably realizing that it would be useful for others too, decided to release it to the world.

Bringing together their most commonly utilized CSS, jQuery plugins, elements, and best practices, Zurb released the Foundation framework in 2011. With its release came a couple of firsts: the first open-source front-end framework to be **responsive**, and the first to take a **mobile-first** approach, and the first to be *semantic*.

---

[1] http://foundation.zurb.com/docs/

[2] http://zurb.com/

Impressive, right? But what does all that mean? Well, being the **responsive** framework that it is, Foundation-enabled websites have the ability to respond to different screen sizes correctly and smoothly right out of the box. With Foundation, there's no need to worry about styles breaking or elements disappearing when the user's screen size strays from that which you had in mind when developing. Of course, this assumes you've stayed within the comforting arms of the grid layout (more on that later in the book).

Along with the ease of building responsively, Foundation takes a **mobile-first** approach to web design. This means that when you develop projects with the Foundation framework, your design elements are built first with small screens in mind. It then gives you various choices to tweak the layout and rearrange components in larger screens easily without writing much code. With the ever-increasing popularity of mobile browsing, this makes good practice for web development in general.

Finally, as a **semantic** framework, Foundation allows you to use markup that just makes plain sense. This is an often overlooked benefit of the framework, but for a web developer who spends large amounts of time sifting through HTML selectors, having easily readable markup can make a world of difference. In addition, being among the top 15 open-source projects with over 500 contributors at the time of writing, Foundation maintains good code quality and uses the easiest markup for its components.

Proof of Zurb's diligent innovations is evident when browsing the components section of the Foundation documentation.[3] Humorously termed the "kitchen sink," the default Foundation package includes the following components, allowing you to add some traditionally advanced functionality with only a few lines of code:

- Structure—Foundation components that will help in defining the structure of web pages:
  - media queries
  - visibility
  - grid
  - block grid
  - interchange responsive component
  - utility classes

---

[3] http://foundation.zurb.com/docs/components/kitchen_sink.html

  - JavaScript utilities
  - right-to-left support

- Navigation—components that will help in providing effective naviagtion:
  - off-canvas
  - top bar
  - icon bar
  - side nav
  - Magellan sticky nav
  - sub nav
  - breadcrumbs
  - pagination

- Media—components that will be used to hold images and videos:
  - Orbit slider
  - thumbnails
  - clearing lightbox
  - flex video

- Forms—Foundation provides many pre-styled form elements that will help in enhacing the user experience of our web forms:
  - forms
  - switches
  - range sliders
  - Abide validation

- Buttons—beautifully designed action elements (links and buttons):
  - buttons
  - button groups
  - split buttons
  - drop-down buttons

- Typography—components that will help to enhance the look of some text elements such as important notices, list items, and so on in our web pages:
  - type
  - inline lists
  - labels
  - keystrokes

- Callouts and prompts—components that will help in gaining the user's attention to convey important messages:
  - reveal modal
  - alerts
  - panels
  - tooltips
  - Joyride
- Content—useful components that are commonly found on the Web:
  - drop-downs
  - pricing tables
  - progress bars
  - tables
  - accordion
  - tabs
  - equalizer

As you can see, Foundation comes equipped with a lot of useful components out of the box! We'll go through many of these components in detail in later chapters, understanding how they are made and what HTML markup is needed to create them on our web pages.

These components come prebuilt and configured to be inserted seamlessly into a Foundation-enabled web project. All that's required of you, beyond the few lines of code needed to include these components, is to customize them as you see fit. Which brings me to my next point on Foundation: just about everything within the Foundation framework is completely customizable, from global styles to the minutiae of component behavior. You can change everything about it to tailor it for your own needs.

With all these impressive features going for it, how can the Foundation framework have any competition? Well, I'm glad you asked. Today, there are many open-source front-end frameworks available for us to use. Some of the most popular ones are:

- Bootstrap[4]

---

[4] http://getbootstrap.com

- Yahoo Pure[5]
- Google Web Starter Kit[6]
- UIkit[7]
- Semantic UI[8]
- Ink[9]
- Concise[10]

Feel free to browse each of the above frameworks to discover what predeveloped components they have to offer.

Let's compare Foundation with arguably its biggest competitor, Bootstrap. Like a fine scotch whiskey, the question of which framework reigns supreme can largely be boiled down to personal preference. Once you know one framework, there is little difference compared to the others. Many classes used in these frameworks are intuitive; you just have to recognize their naming scheme.

Here's a quick rundown of the major attributes of the two most popular CSS frameworks:

	Foundation	**Bootstrap**
Basic structure	grid	grid
Sizing units	rem	pixel
License	Open source (MIT)	Open source (MIT)
CSS preprocessor	Sass	LESS/Sass
Grid columns	12	12
Number of components	a whole lot	Also a whole lot

Though this is admittedly a basic overview of the two frameworks, it's evident that they share more in common than not. Just about anything you can do with Bootstrap you can just as easily accomplish with Foundation, and vice versa. The biggest

---

[5] http://purecss.io/
[6] https://developers.google.com/web/starter-kit/
[7] http://getuikit.com/
[8] http://semantic-ui.com/
[9] http://ink.sapo.pt/
[10] http://concisecss.com/

points of difference revolve around CSS compilation and the way they approach grid layouts.

We should remember that customization is an important factor in selecting a framework. Foundation provides customization through Sass only whereas Bootstrap lets you customize its CSS through both Sass and LESS. If you are unfamiliar with LESS/Sass, they are CSS preprocessors that bring logic and functional ability to CSS. The preprocesser code needs to compiled into static CSS files that will be used in our websites. We'll learn more about customizing Foundation frameworks through Sass in Chapter 7. Meanwhile, check out the official websites of LESS[11] and Sass[12] to learn more about them.

Up until version 3 of Bootstrap, if you preferred Sass you were forced to use Foundation, while LESS devotees were ushered towards Bootstrap. As of version 3, Bootstrap has successfully been ported to Sass. Foundation, however, still relies upon the Sass language for compiling CSS. If all this talk of CSS compilation makes you dizzy, worry not—we'll cover it in-depth later on. For now, you should simply understand that both frameworks are designed to work with CSS compilers.

Similarly, both CSS frameworks make use of a grid layout for their most basic structure. This means that web projects built with either framework will be equally responsive with only minor syntax differences. Both frameworks default to a 12-column layout that can be extensively customized via Sass or LESS. We will learn more about grid systems in Chapter 2.

In the end, with so much feature overlap, choosing between Foundation and Bootstrap is akin to deciding between red or blue. It all comes down to personal taste. At least it's comforting to know you have options, right? If you do decide ultimately to select Bootstrap over Foundation, you could check out the SitePoint book *Jump Start Bootstrap*[13] by Syed Fazle Rahman.

Setting up a Foundation Project

Installing and configuring Foundation for use in your own projects is as easy as making a few decisions followed by a few clicks. To start, head over to the Zurb

---

[11] http://lesscss.org/

[12] http://sass-lang.com

[13] https://learnable.com/books/jump-start-bootstrap

Foundation website and locate the downloads page.[14] Once there, you'll find a few options that are shown in Figure 1.1.

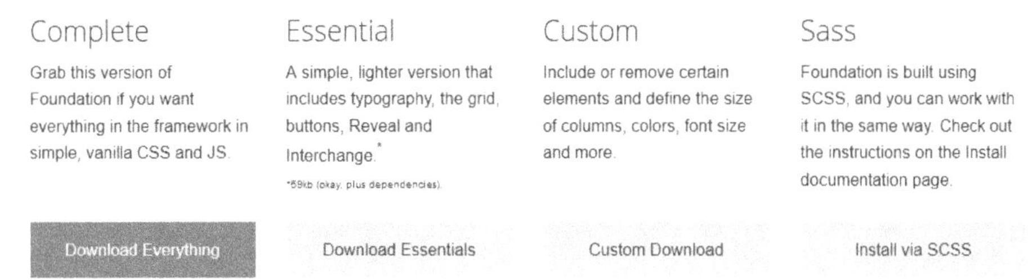

Figure 1.1. Foundation download options

For those just starting out with Foundation, the "Complete" option provides a Foundation package that includes all available components. Think of this option as the most comprehensive Foundation package. Next up, the "Essential" package is a pared-down version of the Foundation experience for those with less ambitious needs of the framework. Included is a much smaller collection of features covering the bare essentials of web development with Foundation. Then again, if you know exactly what you need from the Foundation framework, the "Custom" option will likely serve you well. As its name implies, with this option you can choose which elements you'd like to include in your Foundation package and those you'd like to do without. Not only that, you can also define some global styles such as color, font size, and column size to be built into the resulting package. Finally, those looking to tap into the power and convenience of CSS preprocessing, the "Sass" option will take you to a page with detailed instructions for getting started with Sass.

If you download the "Essential" package, upgrading to the "Complete" package would require including the missing JavaScript files and recompiling the Sass files into CSS. Hence, you need to make sure which version you'd like to go with for your web project before downloading.

For our needs, we'll stick with the first option and download the "Complete" package. What you should end up with after clicking the download link is a ZIP file containing the entire Foundation framework. To install the framework, simply extract the archive to the root directory of your web project. Once extracted, you'll

[14] http://foundation.zurb.com/develop/download.html

find **css**, **img**, and **js** folders along with a few files including the all-important **index.html**, as shown in Figure 1.3. At the time of writing this book, Foundation version 5.5.2 was the latest release, and it is also used throughout this book.

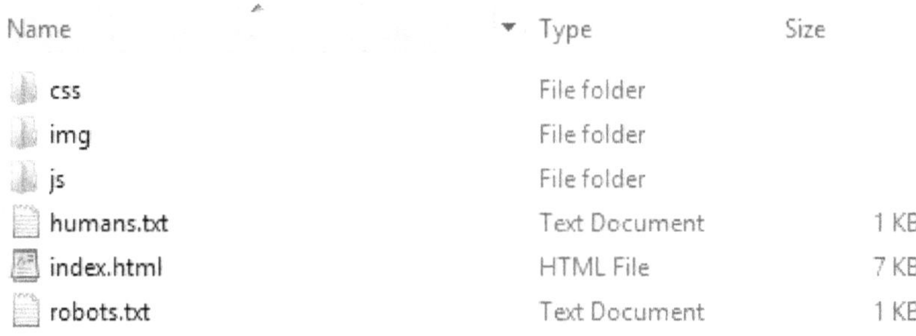

Figure 1.2. The extracted Foundation package

The folders included in the default Foundation package are fairly self-explanatory. The **css** folder contains the predefined Foundation styles as well as any custom stylesheets you decide to add; the **js** folder likewise contains the necessary scripts for all Foundation components; and lastly the **img** folder will contain the images you'll be including in your web project. With those files in place, you're set to go. Yep, it really is that easy! If you don't believe me, go ahead and point your web browser at the directory in which you just extracted the Foundation package. With any luck it should look like Figure 1.3.

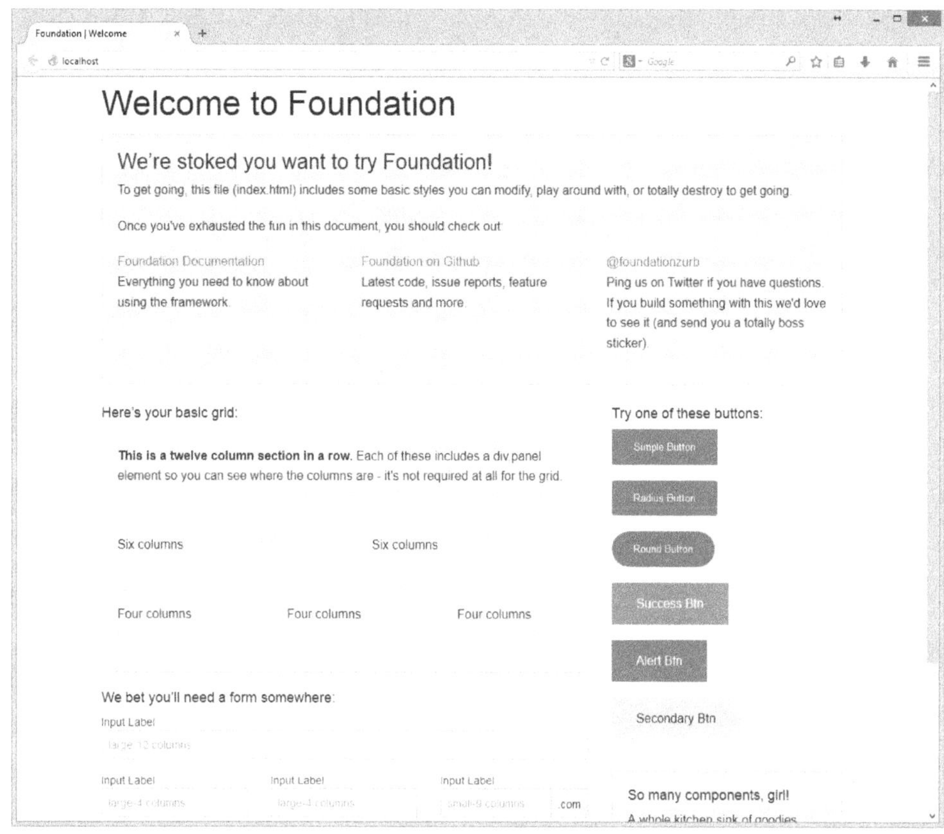

Figure 1.3. Foundation's default index page

Summary

With that, you're fully equipped to tackle the rest of this book. We trust you're not overwhelmed with the wealth of information you've just received, but it is useful to have a firm grasp on what CSS frameworks are and why they're useful to you as a web developer.

Throughout this chapter we've covered the basics of the the Foundation framework, including an example that showed just hwo quickly Foundation can be used to set up a prototype website. We also learned what the Zurb Foundation is. You then saw a quick comparison of Foundation to the other giant in the CSS framework arena, Bootstrap. Finally, we concluded the chapter with a rundown of the steps to set up your first project with the Foundation framework. In truth, it wasn't that many steps at all, but that's a good thing! You're now ready to get your hands dirty and make use of the Foundation framework to build a basic website. What are you waiting for? Head on to Chapter 2!

Chapter 2

Getting Started With Foundation's Grid System

Who doesn't want their websites to look beautiful and well-structured in mobile devices? Considering the plethora of sites vying for users' attention, our website should be ready to modify itself automatically for any kind of display devices. But this sort of website design is challenging and requires many hours of HTML and CSS coding. Foundation framework, on the other hand, gives you the ability to create such responsive websites on the go. You don't have to write a single line of CSS code to make a responsive website.

In this chapter, we are going to explore one of the main concepts in Foundation: the **grid system**—a 12-column flexible grid that can scale to any size. We'll see how to implement it and make our websites mobile-friendly and well-structured.

Laying the Foundation

As you learned in Chapter 1, Foundation's main goal is to provide you with a framework from which to build upon. The way that Foundation accomplishes this goal is with the grid layout. Before we go any further, let's take a step back and look at how web designs are structured.

Long ago in a galaxy far, far away, when web development was very much in its infancy, designs typically consisted of free-flowing paragraph elements. The result looked more like a dishevelled newspaper page than the sophisticated, media-rich designs we see today.

In an attempt to bring order to the chaos, HTML tables were utilized. While they certainly helped clean up the mess, their rigidity cast a distinct coldness to the face of the early Web. Here are a few reasons why HTML tables are bad for layouts:

- Tables used this way describe presentation rather than content, hence a website laid out using tables is semantically incorrect.
- Screen-reader users find it difficult to understand websites that use tables for layout.
- It is very difficult to redesign a website using a table layout.
- Tables can break text copying, which can be very annoying for some users.

Apologies for the history lesson on web design, but it serves as a good illustration for why Foundation (as well as other popular CSS frameworks) chose a grid layout for its most basic building block. You see, in general the Web is a giant repository for content to be consumed. As humans we're used to consuming our content in an orderly fashion. Grid layouts grant that ability in a very flexible way.

Striking a wonderful balance between the rigidity of tables and the freedom of home-grown CSS, the grid represents the bedrock of the Foundation framework. Figure 2.1 shows a quick example of what the grid layout looks like in practice:

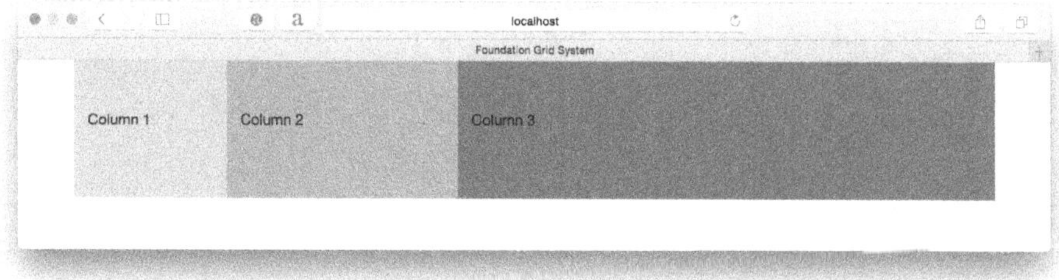

Figure 2.1. A basic example of the Foundation grid system

You can see there is a single row containing three columns of different colors and widths. This is the most basic use of Foundation's grid system. Let's add a new row and insert two columns of different widths within it, seen in Figure 2.2.

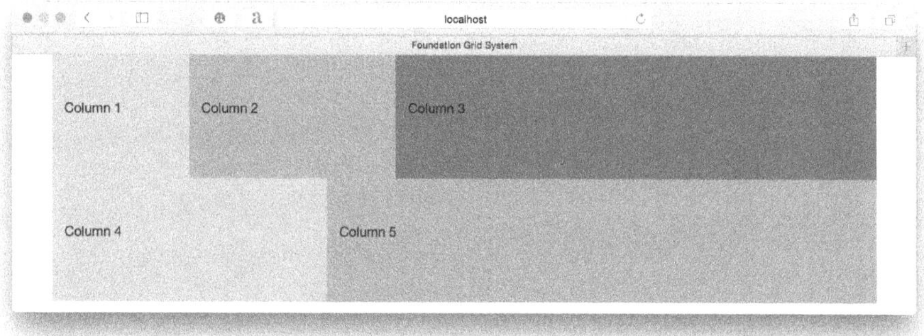

Figure 2.2. Extending our example with two rows

The point to be noted here is that our website is shown on a desktop-sized browser. What will happen once we reduce the size of the browser window, such as on a mobile device? The screenshot in Figure 2.3 shows our website in a smaller browser window.

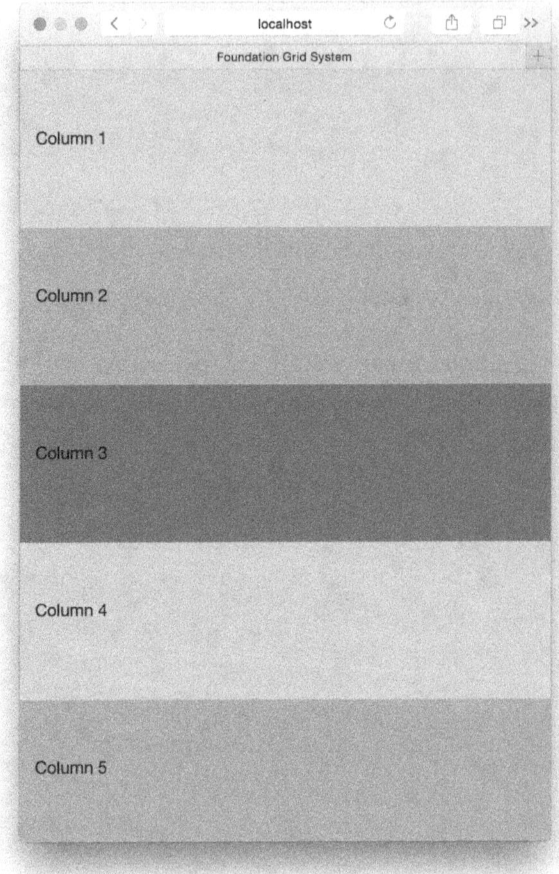

Figure 2.3. Our simple example in a narrower window

Oh. That was unexpected. How did two different rows with multiple columns end up stacked on top of each other? Let's aim to understand by checking out the code in the following sections.

Setting up a Foundation Project

Before we start coding, we'll set up our project with the Foundation framework. In Chapter 1, we saw that we determine what version of Foundation to download depending on our need. For the sake of understanding Foundation in this book, we'll use the static Complete Foundation 5 version,[1] which has all the static, compiled CSS files. Let's create a new folder called **Foundation Grid System Lessons** in our system. Copy all the files from the downloaded Foundation project into this folder, then open **index.html** using your favorite code editor. My favorite is GitHub's Atom editor,[2] but you can use whatever you like.

Index.html should look like this:

index.html *(excerpt)*

```
<!doctype html>
<!--[if IE 9]><html class="lt-ie10" lang="en" > <![endif]-->
<html class="no-js" lang="en">
    <head>
        <meta charset="utf-8" />
        <meta name="viewport" content="width=device-width,
➥ initial-scale=1.0" />

        <title>Foundation Grid System</title>
        <link rel="stylesheet" href="css/foundation.css" />

        <script src="js/vendor/modernizr.js"></script>
    </head>
    <body>

        <!-- Your code goes here -->

        <script src="js/vendor/jquery.js"></script>
        <script src="js/foundation.min.js"></script>

        <script>
        $(document).foundation();
        </script>
    </body>
</html>
```

This is the recommended markup for use with Foundation. Whenever you start a new project, you should set your **index.html** file up this way so that it has the correct structure.

---

[1] http://foundation.zurb.com/develop/download.html

[2] https://atom.io

The first item to notice in this code is the commented `<html>` tag at the beginning. This is a method of detecting older Internet Explorer browsers, as Foundation is incompatible with browsers below IE9. This tag adds a class `lt-ie10` to the `<html>` tag, so if you want to add custom CSS styles for older versions of IE, you can attach them to this CSS class.

Next, we have two meta tags that tell browsers how to interpret and represent a particular website. The first meta tag tells the browser the textual character set used in this website. In this case, we're using character set UTF-8.[3]

The second meta tag is a `viewport` tag, which tells the browser how to render a particular website. In our case, we are indicating for the browser to use all the available browser space and make our website width equal to the browser width. This is important because some mobile browsers have problems rendering websites that are responsive; that is, websites that modify their layout with respect to the size of the browser.

Then we include Foundation's default CSS file by specifying the path to the `<link>` tag. We've also added a third-party JavaScript library called `modernizr.js`. As the Foundation framework has used many newer HTML5 tags and CSS3 features, this library helps to detect if the browser supports these features and then adds conditional code to the website. You can read more about Modernizr on its official website.[4]

Inside the `<body>` section, we've included two JavaScript files: **jquery.js** and **foundation.min.js**. Since Foundation depends on jQuery, you must *always* include jQuery before including Foundation's JavaScript file. Finally, we have initialized Foundation's script by calling the `foundation()` method. This function initializes all the predefined JavaScript components in Foundation that we'll cover in future chapters.

---

[3] http://en.wikipedia.org/wiki/UTF-8

[4] http://modernizr.com

Getting Our Hands Dirty with the Grid System

Before creating any columns, we first need the rows that will hold them. Let's create a row first:

```
<div class="row">
</div>
```

It's that simple. You just add the class `row` to the `<div>` element to create a row.

The Foundation grid system divides the screen into 12 equally sized columns by default. These are called **virtual columns** and their widths vary as per the width of the device. The real columns are created by specifying how many of the 12 Foundation virtual columns you wish to span with your columns. Suppose we want only a single column. Then we'll span all the 12 available virtual Foundation columns. For this we'll use the class `large-12`. (You can ignore the `large` term in the class name for now; we'll discuss that later).

The code for creating a single column that spans all twelve virtual Foundation columns looks like this:

```
<div class="row">
    <div class="column large-12">
    </div>
</div>
```

In Foundation, it's mandatory to attach an additional class `column` to every column element, as it helps Foundation to easily identify a column. You can also use the class `columns` instead of `column` and Foundation will create the same column for you. There's no difference between `columns` and `column`.

Let's proceed to create a two-column layout. if we want to have two equal-width columns, each will occupy six virtual Foundation columns:

index.html *(excerpt)*

```
<div class="row">
    <div class="large-6 column" style="background: #aaaaaa; height:
➥ 100px;">
        Column 1
    </div>
    <div class="large-6 column" style="background: #cccccc; height:
➥ 100px;">
        Column 2
    </div>
</div>
```

I have added background colors and height to each column so that we can clearly distinguish between them. Let's check out how this looks in a browser, in Figure 2.4.

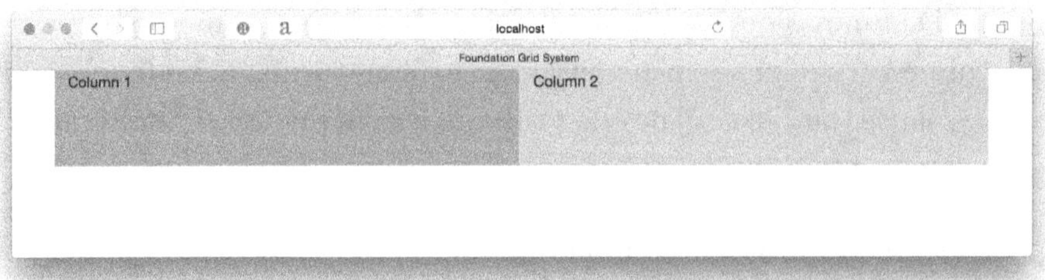

Figure 2.4. A basic two-column layout

Easy enough? Let's add another row and this time create three different-width columns in it. You can see the result in Figure 2.5:

index.html *(excerpt)*

```
<div class="row">
    <div class="large-2 column" style="background: #bbbbbb;height:
➥ 100px;">
        Column 3
    </div>
    <div class="large-7 column" style="background: #dddddd;height:
➥ 100px;">
        Column 4
    </div>
    <div class="large-3 column" style="background: #aaaaaa;height:
➥ 100px;">
```

```
        Column 5
    </div>
</div>
```

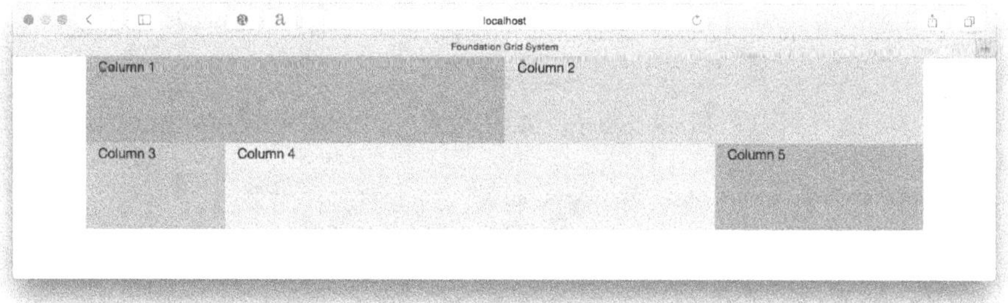

Figure 2.5. Two rows: one with two equal-width columns, one with three columns of different widths

Only 12 Virtual Columns Per Row

The sum total of the number of virtual columns allocated to each column should always be equal to 12 in every row. If the sum exceeds 12, Foundation automatically creates a new row and shifts the extra columns to this new row. Try it out yourself by allocating a larger number of the virtual columns to the last column in the previous example.

Foundation also lets you nest these columns; in other words, insert a new row inside the columns. All you have to do is create a new `row` inside any `column` element and then start inserting columns into it. The only difference here is that the width of the row will depend on the width of the parent column. Let's code a nested column:

index.html *(excerpt)*

```
<div class="row">
    <div class="large-6 column" style="background: #aaaaaa;height:
➥ 100px;">
        Column 1

        <!-- Nested Columns -->
        <div class="row">
            <div class="large-8 column" style="background: #888;
➥height: 60px;">
                Nested Column 1
```

```
            </div>
            <div class="large-4 column" style="background: #999;
➥height: 60px;">
                  Nested Column 2
            </div>
         </div>

      </div>
      <div class="large-6 column" style="background: #cccccc;height:
➥ 100px;">
         Column 2
      </div>
</div>
```

This code will look as it does in Figure 2.6.

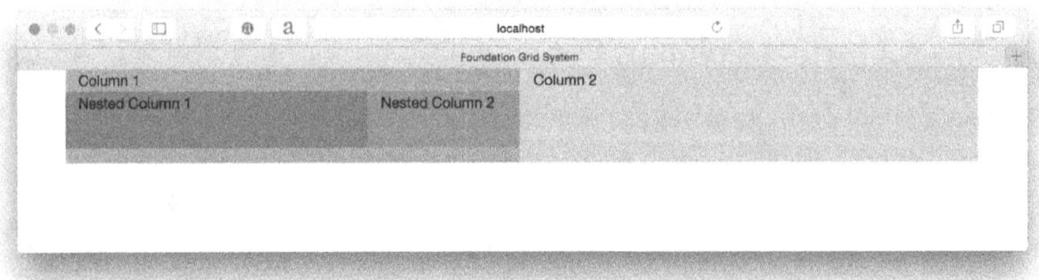

Figure 2.6. Nested columns

Offsets

The final thing to discuss with regard to Foundation's grid is using **offsets**. Foundation lets you shift any column upto 11 virtual columns towards the right. Let's imagine a new situation now where we want to create a single column that spans across six virtual Foundation columns and it should be center aligned with respect to the browser window. So, in order to center a column occupying six virtual columns, we'll need to shift it three virtual columns towards the right. This is done by adding classes like `.large-offset-*` to the column elements, where `*` represents number of virtual Foundation columns you want to offset. Here's the code to center a column that spans across six virtual Foundation columns:

index.html *(excerpt)*

```
<div class="row">
    <div class="large-6 large-offset-3 column" style="background:
➥#ddd;height: 200px; margin-top: 50px;">
        Hello World.
    </div>
</div>
```

This will create a centered column, as shown in Figure 2.7.

Figure 2.7. A column centered using offsets

Foundation's Responsive Nature

The world of web design is quite different today than it was even five years ago. A few factors have played prominent roles in ushering the sweeping changes to the design landscape that we've seen, but the most conspicuous is the natural progression of technology. Web technologies are refined, bandwidth increases, and the devices we use to consume web content become more capable. In recent times, this change has presented a unique challenge. For a long time, the interfaces (or screens) we used to view web content steadily grew in size, the modern proliferation of mobile devices has lead to increased browsing on considerably smaller screens.

Instead of focusing on a select few popular and large desktop screen sizes, modern developers have had to produce equally capable designs for small screens as well. The difficulties in translating media-rich large-screen experiences to the much smaller mobile screen led to the development of **Responsive Web Design** (RWD).

In short, web content that is designed responsively will react intelligently and dynamically to differing screen sizes. Pages dynamically restructure themselves to present content in the most meaningful way based on the user's screen size.

With the Foundation framework, each page you design will be inherently responsive when built within the grid layout. To prove that I'm not just pulling your leg, let's take a look at the two-row grid-layout examples we created in the previous section. You'll remember that we didn't explicitly define any responsive style or behavior in either grid example; we simply added rows and columns. Let's take a look at Figure 2.8 to see what happens when we shrink the screen size.

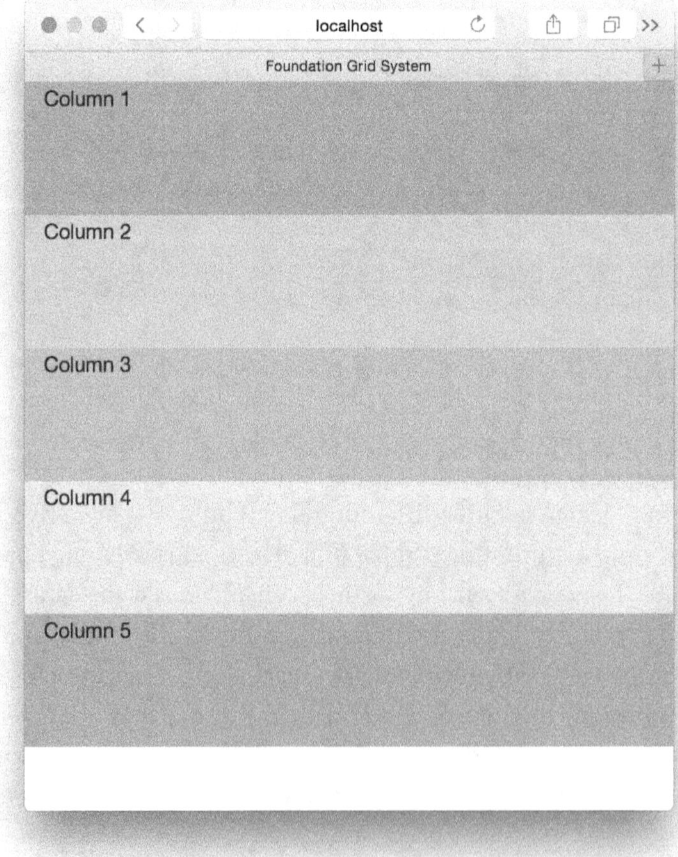

Figure 2.8. Our two-row layout on a smaller screen

Without adding any custom styles, our simple grid layouts have automatically responded to the changing screen size, and the rows and columns have stacked on top of each other. This again illustrates the power of using a framework such as Foundation. Time-consuming aspects of the web development process are made automatic. Yet as well as being automatic, they're also robust, leaving plenty of room for customization and expansion.

Although by default Foundation was able to take care of mobile compatibility, that design might not be what we're after. We may want our columns to adapt differently according to whether the website is to be displayed on mobiles, tablets, and desktop displays. For this situation, Foundation has defined a set of classes for mobiles and tablets. Let's examine them carefully.

For devices with screens less than 640px in width, Foundation has a set of classes that start with `small-#`. And for devices whose widths are more than 640px and less than 1024px, it has classes `medium-#`. The `large-#` classes that we used in the previous section are applicable for devices that are above 1024px in width. This means that it's unnecessary to modify the code we wrote in the previous section to cater for tablets and smartphones separately. We simply add more sizing classes to make columns display differently.

Let's modify the code of the first row as follows:

index.html *(excerpt)*

```
<div class="row">
    <div class="large-6 medium-4 small-12 column" style="background:
➥ #aaaaaa; height: 100px;">
        Column 1
    </div>
    <div class="large-6 medium-8 small-12 column" style="background:
➥ #cccccc; height: 100px;">
        Column 2
    </div>
</div>
```

Here are screenshots on three browser widths.

Figure 2.9 shows that on a desktop screen, it looks the same as previously.

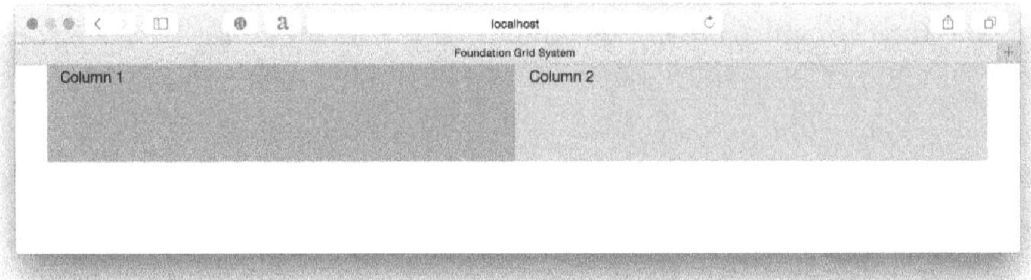

Figure 2.9. Our modified example on a larger screen

In Figure 2.10, we can see what it looks like on a tablet-size browser. The first column is slightly smaller than the second column.

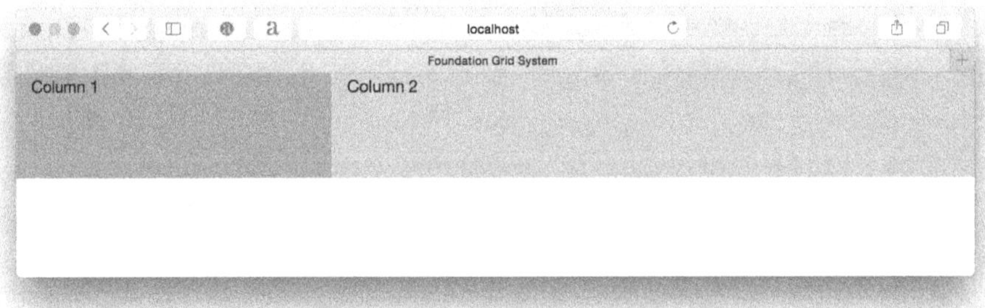

Figure 2.10. Our modified example on a tablet-size screen

On a mobile-size browser, it looks like Figure 2.11. Both columns occupy all the portions of a row, and hence they stack on top of each other.

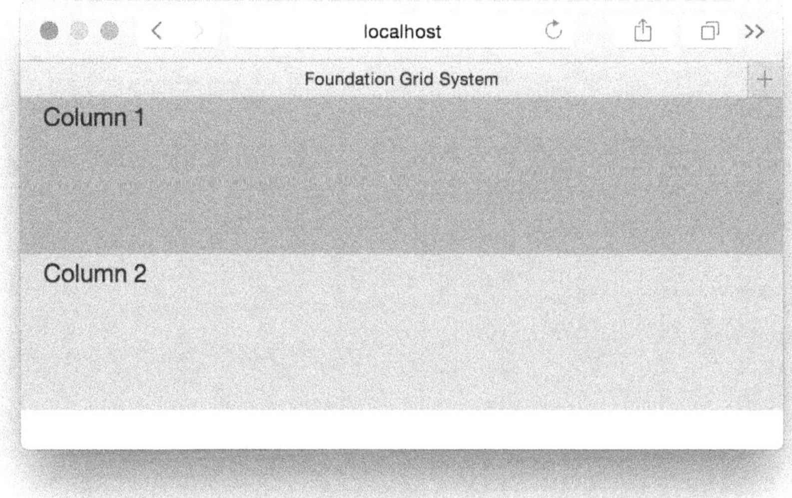

Figure 2.11. Our example on a smartphone-size screen

Foundation also has offset classes that you can use to define specific offsets on small- and medium-sized screens: `small-offset-*` and `medium-offset-*` respectively.

Summary

In this chapter, we went over the basics of site layouts with Foundation. You learned all about the grid system and how to use its row and column structure to lay an inherently responsive foundation for your designs. Not only that, but you also learned how to take advantage of row nesting to squeeze the most out of your Foundation grid layouts. The knowledge you've gained will be used at the core of each and every Foundation project you create and is critical in the production of well-executed designs.

In the latter half of this chapter, we also dived headfirst into Foundation's responsive nature and the ideas and methodologies behind it.

Chapter 3

Laying Out a Prototype

In the previous chapter, we covered the basics of web design with the Zurb Foundation framework. These included structuring with grid layouts, nesting rows, and responsive design using mobile-first practices and media queries.

Here in Chapter 3, we'll see how to create a simple prototype in Foundation. At the end of this chapter you'll understand why prototyping is useful and know how to prototype effectively with Foundation. You'll also have learned the best practices of web development for multiple screen sizes. Ready?

The Importance of a Good Prototype

Prototyping, the process of creating a sample or model to test concepts, is a technique used to speed up the development process. Prototyping is far from unique to the web development industry. On the contrary, it's been widely used in nearly every industry with development processes for hundreds of years.

So why is it such an important aspect of web development? The answer is twofold: The first reason has everything to do with speeding up the development life cycle.

The second (and equally important) reason involves improving the quality of your resultant applications and designs.

A good way to conceptualize prototyping is to think about the car sitting in your garage and how it came to be. Through the diligent work of many people, a concept was devised, sketched, modeled, prototyped, and after numerous revisions, produced. Can you imagine if they'd jumped straight from the conceptual model to production? Consider the ensuing recalls and lawsuits! Fortunately, car manufacturers work in a much more intelligent way, using prototyping to work out the bugs before you jump behind the wheel.

Now that we have a solid understanding of why prototyping is a good idea, let's dive in and see what it looks like in action.

Building a Basic Prototype

In this chapter, we'll apply the concepts we learn by building a fictitious website for an online photo journal.

As explained in Chapter 2, we'll use the basic Foundation markup to start this project:

```
<!doctype html>
<html class="no-js" lang="en">
    <head>
        <meta charset="utf-8" />
        <meta name="viewport" content="width=device-width,
➥ initial-scale=1.0" />
        <title>Foundation | Welcome</title>
        <link rel="stylesheet" href="css/foundation.css" />
        <script src="js/vendor/modernizr.js"></script>
    </head>
    <body>

        <script src="js/vendor/jquery.js"></script>
        <script src="js/foundation.min.js"></script>
        <script>
            $(document).foundation();
```

```
        </script>
    </body>
</html>
```

Let's begin using the framework by adjusting the title of our prototype in the `<head>` element. We'll name it "Photo Journal" to better reflect the purpose of our project.

Loading up our project in the browser at this point would yield a rather empty page with a simple title in the page's tab, so let's fix that. We'll start by tackling the first section of our prototype: an attention-grabbing full-screen image with overlaying text. We should be sure to make the image height and width fill the entire screen, as we want our users to experience a page-turning effect when they first land onat our site. Regardless of the size of their own screens, when users scroll down they should immediately see content revealed underneath this section. If that doesn't quite make sense, you'll get the idea soon enough when we edit the governing CSS.

As was mentioned earlier, to build web projects with Foundation one need only add rows, columns, and content. It's that easy. So let's add our first row in a div with the class `header`. This is the basic code for creating rows in Foundation:

```
<div class="header">
    <div class="row">
    </div>
</div>
```

In truth, this page would look no different in a browser than it did before we added the row, which is why we'll add the columns and content now. As we know, the default width for a row is twelve virtual columns. You can use as many or as few of those columns as you'd like.

Remember, the goal for our header is to create a full-page image with overlayed text. We'll accomplish the full-page image by specifying a background in the CSS, but to accommodate the overlay text we'll need to make use of Foundation's columns with an offset to push it to the right of the image. Here's the code we'll use:

```
<div class="medium-4 medium-offset-8 columns">
    <h4>Photo Journey</h4>
    <p>Picturing the world one photo at a time.</p>
</div>
```

As shown in Figure 3.1, we created a four-virtual-column-wide element with the class `medium-4`, and used an offset to tell Foundation to push that four-column-wide element eight columns to the right with `medium-offset-8`. This essentially creates an element that is one-third the width of our page, aligned to the right.

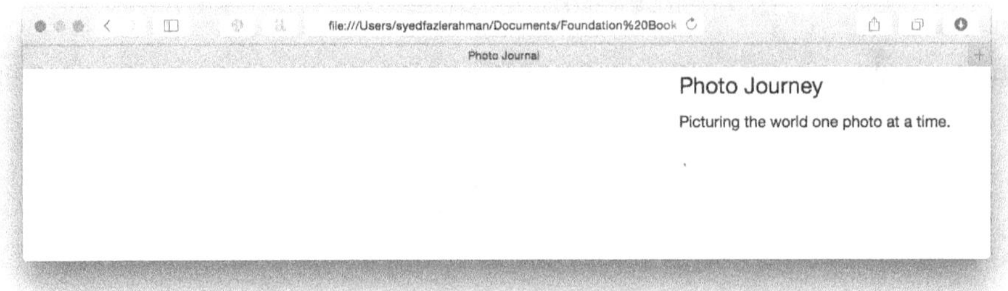

Figure 3.1. Our header overlay in place

Now that the overlay text is in place, let's add the full-page image beneath it. To accomplish this, we'll work some CSS magic to ensure that the image always fills the width and height of the page, regardless of the screen's actual size. I'll also take this opportunity to cover best practices for editing the CSS of your Foundation projects.

If you take a look at the root directory where you extracted the Foundation package, you'll notice an aptly named **css** folder containing predefined styles for the Foundation framework. While you could, in theory, edit these rather large stylesheets directly to add your own custom stylings, it's far easier and prudent to add a new stylesheet called **app.css** to this folder. It's in this file that you should add all custom stylings, as encouraged by the folks at Zurb. Keeping custom CSS styles separate also makes upgrading the Foundation Framework easier and hassle-free.

Let's do this now. Open up the created **app.css** file and add the following:

```
.header {
    height: 100%;
    background: url("http://placehold.it/1920x1080") center
➥ no-repeat;
}

.header .row {
```

```
    padding-top: 30%;
    color: #ffffff;
}
```

The first CSS rule in this code creates a new background for our `header` div. It sets the height to fill the entirety of the page as well as a background image to go with it. Here we're using the placehold.it[1] tool that returns an image of the specified size. You can replace this with an image of your choice.

The second CSS rule modifies the rows we create within our `header` div. In this case it's the overlay text. We set some breathing room at the top and change the color of our text to white so that it stands out over the background image. Before we load this into our browser, we need to ensure that our new stylesheet is loaded correctly in our **index.html**. Here's our **index.html** so far:

index.html *(excerpt)*

```
<!doctype html>
<html class="no-js" lang="en">
    <head>
        <meta charset="utf-8" />
        <meta name="viewport" content="width=device-width,
➥ initial-scale=1.0" />
        <title>Photo Journal</title>
        <link rel="stylesheet" href="css/foundation.css" />
        <link rel="stylesheet" href="css/app.css" />
        <script src="js/vendor/modernizr.js"></script>
    </head>
    <body>
        <div class="header">
            <div class="row">
                <div class="medium-4 medium-offset-8 columns">
                    <h4>Photo Journey</h4>
                    <p>Picturing the world one photo at a time.</p>
                </div>
            </div>
        </div>

        <script src="js/vendor/jquery.js"></script>
        <script src="js/foundation.min.js"></script>
```

[1] http://placehold.it/

```
        <script>
            $(document).foundation();
        </script>
    </body>
</html>
```

If you take a look at our prototype in the browser, you should see a similar sight to Figure 3.2.

Figure 3.2. Our prototype showing background image and overlay

Notice that as you resize the browser window, the background image responds accordingly and the overlay floats neatly in the lower right-hand side of the screen.

We're making great progress so far, so let's move right along to the part of the prototype where the bulk of our content will live. We'll start by adding that content into two new div elements with the class `section`. These elements will house the actual content of our page, and we'll leverage these elements in our **app.css** to customize our content accordingly.

Go ahead and add two of these divs to your **index.html**, just underneath the `header` div:

```
<div class="section">
</div>

<div class="section">
</div>
```

Figure 3.3 shows a wireframe of how we'll lay out the first section.

Figure 3.3. A wireframe of our first content section

As shown in Figure 3.3, for our first `section` element, we'll add three rows that each hold a different set of content. Just as before, adding new rows to our grid is as easy as this:

```
<div class="row">
</div>
```

Inside the first row let's create a new five-columns-wide element, along with one that's seven columns wide to fill out the width of the row:

```
<div class="medium-5 columns">
</div>
<div class="medium-7 columns">
</div>
```

The first part of this section will serve as a photo diary of sorts with an image in the five-columns-wide element accompanying a journal entry in the seven-columns-wide element. All we have to do is add the desired content between these divs and we're good to go. Let's add a couple more rows underneath to fill out the page. For our second row, we'll do the inverse of what we did in the first. Simply split the row by seven columns, then five columns:

```
<div class="medium-7 columns">
</div>
<div class="medium-5 columns">
</div>
```

This arrangement of vertical elements will help break up our grid and create a more interesting content flow. Let's now edit our last row in this first section and use all twelve columns of the grid width:

```
<div class="large-12 columns">
</div>
```

For this row, we'll use Foundation block grid elements to evenly space horizontal content within the row. To do this we create an unordered list with a list item for each element in the row. When we create the list we specify a class of `"small-block-grid-1 medium-block-grid-3"`, which tells the framework to split the row into three columns on medium and large screen sizes and one column on small screens. Here's the resulting code:

```
<ul class="small-block-grid-1 medium-block-grid-3">
    <li></li>
    <li></li>
    <li></li>
</ul>
```

And with that we're done with our first content section! The final code should look like this (filler content has been added to the elements):

index.html *(excerpt)*

```
<div class="section">
    <div class="row">
        <div class="medium-5 columns">
            <img src="http://placehold.it/500x300">
        </div>
        <div class="medium-7 columns">
            <h5>On this day...</h5>
            <p>Lorem ipsum dolor sit amet, cu case duis pri, vide
➥ melius an per. Ad sed ignota nominavi reprimique. ...</p>
        </div>
    </div>
    <div class="row">
        <div class="medium-7 columns">
            <h5>One year ago...</h5>
            <p>Lorem ipsum dolor sit amet, cu case duis pri, vide
➥ melius an per. Ad sed ignota nominavi reprimique. ...</p>
        </div>
        <div class="medium-5 columns">
            <img src="http://placehold.it/500x300">
        </div>
    </div>
    <div class="row">
        <div class="large-12 columns">
            <ul class="small-block-grid-1 medium-block-grid-3">
                <li><h5>Day One</h5><img src="
➥http://placehold.it/300x150"></li>
                <li><h5>Day Two</h5><img src="
➥http://placehold.it/300x150"></li>
                <li><h5>Day Three</h5><img src="
➥http://placehold.it/300x150"></li>
            </ul>
        </div>
    </div>
</div>
```

To ensure that the rows within our section have plenty of breathing room, let's add some `margin-top` space in our **app.css**:

css/app.css *(excerpt)*

```
.section .row {
    margin-top: 50px;
}
```

The rendered **index.html** should now give you a sight similar to Figure 3.4.

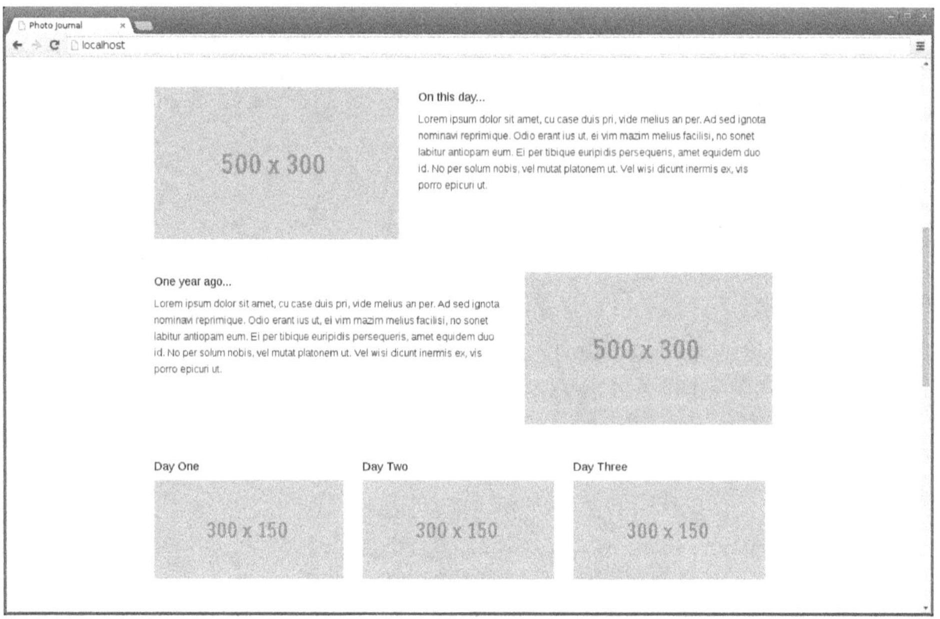

Figure 3.4. Our first content section

Keeping our brisk pace, let's go ahead and add our second section now. For this section, we'll see how easy it is to create responsive media elements; in this case, a video section. We'll make use of Foundation's flex-video component, which lets the framework deal with tasks such as handling aspect ratio and video scaling as screen sizes change (we'll take a closer look at flex video in Chapter 5). We can start by adding a new row to the second `section` div:

```
<div class="section">
    <div class="row">
    </div>
</div>
```

With our empty section and row set up, let's add a full 12-column-wide element with a new flex-video component inside:

```
<div class="large-12 columns">
    <div class="flex-video widescreen vimeo">
        <iframe src="http://player.vimeo.com/video/23205323"
➥width="400" height="225" frameborder="0" webkitAllowFullScreen
➥mozallowfullscreen allowFullScreen></iframe>
    </div>
</div>
```

If you're wondering right now if that's all the code necessary to add responsive video to your Foundation project, let me put your thoughts at ease. It certainly is! All we had to do was create a new div element with a class of `flex-video` (the `widescreen` and `vimeo` attributes are simply for styling purposes) and add an iframe for the video content within.

Looking at our second content section in the browser reveals a clean video element that responds accurately to screen size changes, as shown in Figure 3.5.

Figure 3.5. Our second content section

We've now created two content sections underneath our full-page header, but we still need to direct the flow of our content. Let's create a new content element to separate the sections of our page. To do this we'll create a div with the class `separator`, which will serve as our container. Within this separator element we'll add a new row with a full 12-column container. The idea of these separators is to create a simple block of visual real estate with text describing the section that follows

Here's the **index.html** code for the separator between our two main sections:

index.html *(excerpt)*

```
<div class="separator">
    <div class="row">
            <div class="large-12 columns">
                <h3>Pictures in motion</h3>
                <p>Lorem ipsum dolor sit amet, cu case duis pri,
➥ vide melius an per. Ad sed ignota nominavi reprimique. ... </p>
            </div>
    </div>
</div>
```

Let's make sure this new separator element of ours has an appropriate height and stretches the full width of the page and add a couple styles to our **app.css**. We'll add some breathing room for our separator row, as well as adjust the text color. Then we'll set the `max-width` and `min-height` of our separator container, and set a background color to help differentiate the sections. You'll notice that we steer clear of specifying exact widths and heights, instead relying on relative percentages and min/max values. This is in an effort to preserve the responsiveness of our site:

css/app.css *(excerpt)*

```
.separator .row {
    margin-top: 50px;
    padding-top: 50px;
    color: #ffffff;
}

.separator {
    max-width: 100%;
```

```
    min-height: 50%;
    background-color: #cccccc;
}
```

Opening up our new **index.html** in the browser should yield the same two sections as before; however, they're now separated by a new element with some text giving context to the section that follows, shown in Figure 3.6. Remember, this is just a prototype we're building, so production content is the last thing on our minds. Simple filler images and text are all that's required to give us a good idea of what the page will look like.

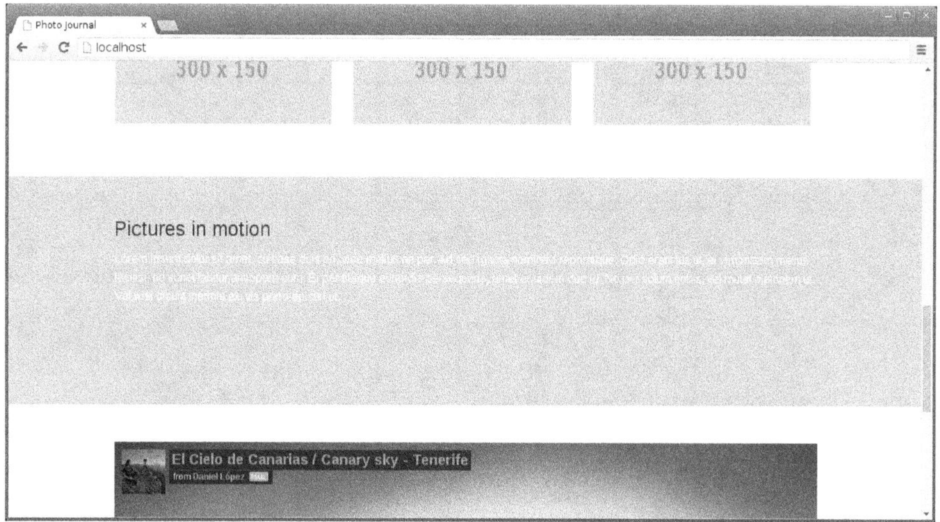

Figure 3.6. Our separator element in place

And with that we've finished both the header and main content sections of our prototype. All that's left is to add a footer element to the bottom of our page. For our footer, we'll make use of the Foundation icon bar component to place a ribbon at the bottom of our page with universal icons directing users towards forms of site communication. The beauty of the icon bar lies in its ability to present navigation with images instead of text. Not only that, but it's incredibly easy to set up. All we do is create a new icon bar div with an attribute telling Foundation how many elements to display:

```
<div class="icon-bar five-up">
</div>
```

In our case we'll be using five icons, so we add the `five-up` attribute to divide the space into five equal parts. To add icons to the bar, we create a new anchor with a class item inside this div:

```
<a class="item">
    <i class="fi-mail"></i>
</a>
<a class="item">
    <i class="fi-bookmark"></i>
</a>
<a class="item">
    <i class="fi-social-tumblr"></i>
</a>
<a class="item">
    <i class="fi-social-twitter"></i>
</a>
<a class="item">
    <i class="fi-like"></i>
</a>
```

Figure 3.7 shows the resulting render.

Figure 3.7. The footer in our prototype

Within each of these `item` anchors we add the items themselves, which are simply blank elements with a class corresponding to the Foundation icon we'd like to use. These are font icons provided for free by Zurb. The advantage of using font icons is that they will look crisp in any display resolution. These icons can be found at Foundation's website,[2] and simply need to be downloaded and stored in the **img** folder of your root directory. By adding `href=""` attributes to the anchor tags, we can direct these icons wherever we wish. Just like that, our footer has a beautiful icon bar with elegant (not to mention scalable) icons directing our users to various contact links.

Summary

We meant to suggest that you start a timer or stopwatch at the beginning of this chapter and stop it the second you finished the footer. There's no doubt you'd surprise yourself with just how quickly you set up a fully functional prototype with minimal styling. In fact, most of your time would have been spent reading with actual coding taking up only a fraction of the final time. Regardless, I think it's clear how you can benefit from the Foundation framework in how it speeds up development.

In this chapter, you started with nothing and created a fully styled prototype. You learned how to use the Foundation grid layout and add rows and columns. You even learned how to offset columns to achieve specific horizontal positioning. You had your first encounter with Foundation components and used block grids, flex video, and the icon bar to add advanced functionality.

As one last exercise and illustration of the value Foundation adds to you web projects, go ahead and pull up the prototype in your favorite browser. Looks good, right? Now shrink the right side of your browser window until it's as narrow as it can be. Better yet, bring up the page in your phone's browser. What you see now is a great example of Foundation's inherent responsiveness. Even though we did next to nothing to build in responsive stylings, our prototype is fully functional—even on mobile screens. And we accomplished this with writing only twenty-five lines of CSS!

---

[2] http://zurb.com/playground/foundation-icon-fonts-3

Now that you have a good idea of how powerful and useful Foundation can be, let's dig into some more advanced components in Chapter 4!

Chapter 4

Content Is King

So far in this book, we have learned how to create various types of website layouts using the grid system and have built a simple website prototype.

This chapter is going to be mostly practical. We'll learn how to style and organize the content of our website using alerts, panels, responsive tables, tabs, and navigation bars.

Making the content presentable is a vitally important factor you should consider when building any website. Foundation provides us with many useful pre-built components such as zebra-highlighted tables, beautiful buttons, tooltips, alerts, and panels that we can directly use in our website to showcase and make the most of our content.

Containing Content

This chapter is broadly classified into two categories: Foundation components that **contain content** and components that help in **organizing content**, such as tabs and navigation bars. In this section, we will focus on creating and understanding three CSS components of the Foundation framework that are used for containing content:

1. panels
2. tables
3. alerts

Panels

Foundation's **Panel** component helps in prominently highlighting announcements on a web page. You can use it to deliver notices to the website's visitors. Panels are designed to stand out from the rest of the web page's content.

Panels are one of the simplest CSS components in Foundation. You just add a single CSS class, `panel`, to make a `div` element into a Foundation panel. Here's an example of a panel:

```
<div class="panel">
    <p>Some dummy content. Lorem ipsum dolor sit amet, consectetur
➥ adipiscing elit. Pellentesque nec turpis ex. Sed venenatis magna
➥ ac risus aliquet placerat. </p>
</div>
```

This markup will look similar to Figure 4.1 in a browser.

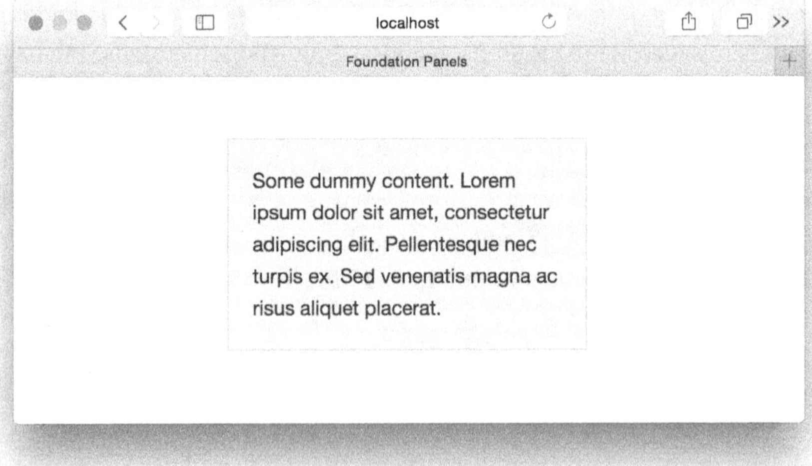

Figure 4.1. A basic example of a panel

There's absolutely no restriction to the type of content you can add inside a panel component. Try adding images and heading tags in it.

Foundation also provides a panel component with a blue background called a **callout panel**. It has a light blue background and a slightly dark blue border around it.

To create a callout panel, you need to add an additional class, `callout`, along with the class `panel`. Let's modify our existing default panel into a callout panel:

```
<div class="panel callout">
    <p>Some dummy content. Lorem ipsum dolor sit amet, consectetur
➥ adipiscing elit. Pellentesque nec turpis ex. Sed venenatis magna
➥ ac risus aliquet placerat. </p>
</div>
```

You can see that the default gray-colored panel is now a blue-colored panel. A callout panel will be useful in situations where the default panel fails to grab your users' attention, perhaps getting lost in your website's color theme.

The border radius of the panel component can be modified by adding Foundation's helper class named `radius`. This adds a border radius of `3px` to all corners of the panel component. Figure 4.2 presents the result of:

panel.html *(excerpt)*

```
<div class="panel callout radius">
    <p>Some dummy content. Lorem ipsum dolor sit amet, consectetur
➥ adipiscing elit. Pellentesque nec turpis ex. Sed venenatis magna
➥ ac risus aliquet placerat. </p>
</div>
```

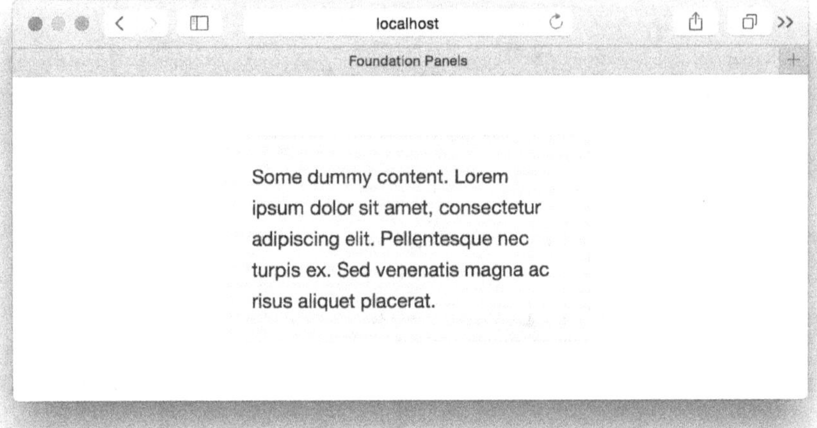

Figure 4.2. A callout panel with a border radius

Panels are Fluid

Panel components have fluid width by default. Their widths are controlled by the grid columns in which they are present.

Radius Won't Work Everywhere

It's worth noting that the useful `radius` helper class won't work for all of Foundation's components. In Foundation, this class works for panels, buttons, and form input elements only. You can, however, create your own custom style by overriding default properties or adding new properties in your **app.css** file.

Tables

Foundation provides some basic styling for the default HTML tables. You don't have to add any classes to apply these styles as this is done by default. Let's create a basic HTML table and check out how it looks in the Foundation framework:

tables.html *(excerpt)*

```
<table>
  <thead>
    <tr>
      <th width="200">Table Header</th>
      <th>Table Header</th>
      <th width="150">Table Header</th>
      <th width="150">Table Header</th>
    </tr>
  </thead>
  <tbody>
    <tr>
      <td>Content Goes Here</td>
      <td>This is longer content Donec id elit non mi porta gravida
➥ at eget metus.</td>
      <td>Content Goes Here</td>
      <td>Content Goes Here</td>
    </tr>
    <tr>
      <td>Content Goes Here</td>
      <td>This is longer Content Goes Here Donec id elit non mi
➥ porta gravida at eget metus.</td>
      <td>Content Goes Here</td>
      <td>Content Goes Here</td>
    </tr>
    <tr>
      <td>Content Goes Here</td>
      <td>This is longer Content Goes Here Donec id elit non mi
➥ porta gravida at eget metus.</td>
      <td>Content Goes Here</td>
      <td>Content Goes Here</td>
    </tr>
  </tbody>
</table>
```

Figure 4.3 shows what it looks like in the browser.

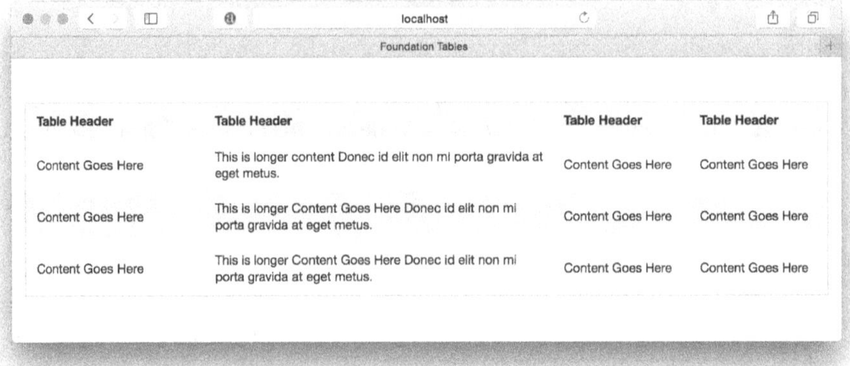

Table Header	Table Header	Table Header	Table Header
Content Goes Here	This is longer content Donec id elit non mi porta gravida at eget metus.	Content Goes Here	Content Goes Here
Content Goes Here	This is longer Content Goes Here Donec id elit non mi porta gravida at eget metus.	Content Goes Here	Content Goes Here
Content Goes Here	This is longer Content Goes Here Donec id elit non mi porta gravida at eget metus.	Content Goes Here	Content Goes Here

Figure 4.3. A default Foundation table

You can see that Foundation applies a light gray color to the table headers and alternative rows (zebra-style). It also adds a border around the table by default.

Unlike many other CSS frameworks, Foundation doesn't provide various types of pre-styled tables; instead, you can customize the default one.

Responsive Foundation Tables

One of the major problems with this default Foundation table is that it fails the responsive test. When there are many columns in the table, it may look broken on smaller screens. There's also no support for responsive tables in the default Foundation framework; however, Foundation has released a separate package for responsive tables as a part of the Foundation Playground[1] website, where they share technical experiments. The package can be downloaded from http://zurb.com/playground/responsive-tables. Copy the files **responsive-tables.css** and **responsive-tables.js** from this package to your project directory, then link the CSS file into the `<head>` section of the HTML file as follows:

```
<link type="text/css" media="screen" rel="stylesheet"
➥href="css/responsive-tables.css" />
```

Now insert the JavaScript file into the HTML file as follows:

[1] http://zurb.com/playground

```
<script type="text/javascript" src="js/responsive-tables.js">
➥</script>
```

Make sure that you add the JavaScript just after the jQuery file, otherwise it will fail to work.

After you have linked these two files, add a class named `responsive` to the `<table>` element. The table will become responsive magically!

Go ahead and add the class `responsive` to the recently created table. Try to resize the browser screen to a smaller size or use Chrome's Mobile Emulation Mode to check the table in smaller devices. You can see that there's a horizontal scroll added to the table that lets you view its whole content. The previously broken table now looks a lot better and is completely accessible.

Alerts

As the name suggests, **Alert** components are used to display alert messages in web applications. They are generally used to communicate success, failure, or warning messages. First, let's create a basic alert box:

```
<div data-alert class="alert-box">
  Alert content goes here.
  <a href="#" class="close">&times;</a>
</div>
```

Figure 4.4 shows what this alert box looks like in the browser.

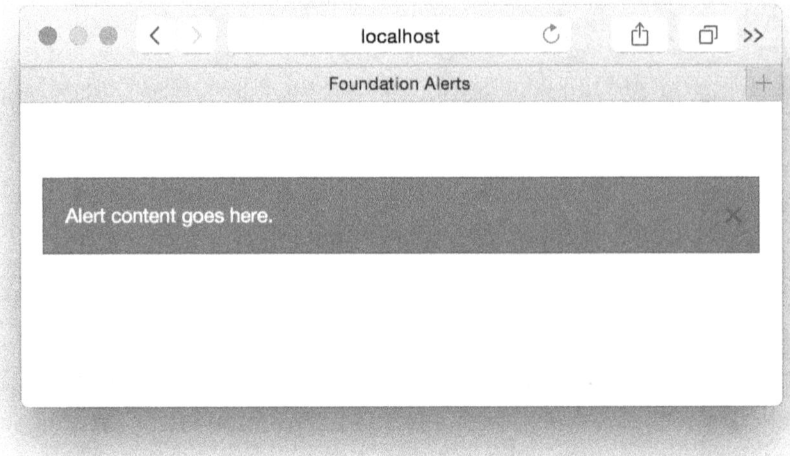

Figure 4.4. A basic alert box

Here, the custom data attribute `data-alert` binds the alert div with Foundation's JavaScript. You also have to add a class named `alert-box` to apply the appropriate CSS styles. Any amount of content can be included inside this alert component; however, you need to add an anchor tag with the class `close` at the end. This tag contains the HTML code `×` for displaying an `x` symbol, which is used to close the alert component. You can also replace it with any font icon of your choice.

Alerts can be used to convey success, failure, or warning messages, as well as display any generic message. Hence, Foundation provides classes to change the color of the alert boxes based on the type of alert.

You can add various classes along with the default class `alert-box` to style the alert. The classes and their colors are as follows:

- `success`: green
- `warning`: orange
- `alert`: red
- `info`: light blue
- `secondary`: gray

Here's an example of an alert box with a color class:

```
<div data-alert class="alert-box success">
  Payment Successful!
  <a href="#" class="close">&times;</a>
</div>
```

You can further enhance the look of the alert box by changing the border radius of the corners. Foundation provides two border classes that work with alert box: `radius` and `round`.

The `radius` class, as we saw in the panels section, adds a border-radius of `3px`, while the `round` class adds a `1000px` border-radius to the alert box. Figure 4.5 shows how they look:

alerts.html *(excerpt)*

```
<div data-alert class="alert-box success radius">
  Alert with .radius class.
  <a href="#" class="close">&times;</a>
</div>

<div data-alert class="alert-box warning round">
```

```
  Alert with .round class.
  <a href="#" class="close">&times;</a>
</div>
```

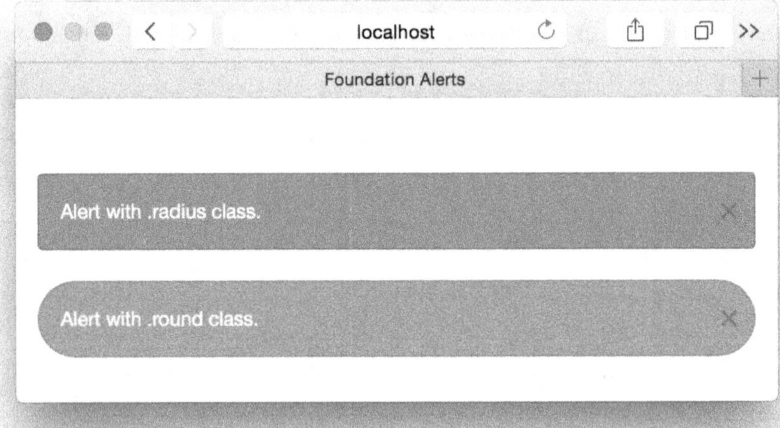

Figure 4.5. Alert boxes using the `round` and `radius` helper classes

As has been mentioned, you can always override the `1000px` border-radius value `round` class in your **app.css** file.

Foundation also provides a custom event, `close.fndtn.alert`, which is fired when the alert is closed. This event can be used to make Ajax calls or perform other client-side operations after the alert is closed. Here's how it is used:

```
$(document).on('close.fndtn.alert', function(event) {
  console.log('Alert closed!');
});
```

Organizing Content

Having well-organized content is vital. You need clean and easy-to-use navigation so that your users can navigate your content. In this section, we are going to learn how to create tabs, drop-downs, and navigation bars using Foundation.

Tabs

Tabs is one of the JavaScript components of Foundation. It allows you to create and organize multiple items in a single container and lets you switch between them easily. Creating a tabs component, just like any other component in Foundation, requires adding only HTML markup.

To create a tabs component, you need two HTML elements: the **tabs section** and the **tabs content**.

The tabs section is created using an unordered list `<ul>` element with the class `tabs` and a custom data attribute named `data-tab`. This custom attribute binds the HTML markup with Foundation's JavaScript:

```
<ul class="tabs" data-tab>
    <li></li>
</ul>
```

Every child `<li>` element in this unordered list represents tabs in the user interface. These `<li>` elements should contain an anchor tag, which will link a tab to a particular content div section. Add the class `tab-title` to each of the `<li>` elements to inherit Foundation's CSS styles. The markup for the tabs section should look a little like this:

tabs.html *(excerpt)*

```
<ul class="tabs" data-tab>
    <li class="tab-title active"><a href="#panel1">Tab 1</a></li>
    <li class="tab-title"><a href="#panel2">Tab 2</a></li>
    <li class="tab-title"><a href="#panel3">Tab 3</a></li>
    <li class="tab-title"><a href="#panel4">Tab 4</a></li>
</ul>
```

You should place an additional class of `active` to one of the `<li>` elements; that will be the tab that's selected when the page loads in the browser. Additionally, the anchor tags should have their `href` attribute set to the IDs of their respective tabs content div sections, which we'll create next.

Creating tabs content requires creating a simple `<div>` element with the class `tabs-content`. This element serves as a parent wrapper for all the child content sections.

Each child <div> element should have a class `content` and a unique ID, corresponding to the links in the tabs section. Here's the markup for the tabs content:

tabs.html *(excerpt)*

```
<div class="tabs-content">

    <div class="content active" id="panel1">
        <p>Lorem ipsum dolor sit amet, consectetur adipiscing elit.
➥ Duis vel aliquet augue.</p>
    </div>

    <div class="content" id="panel2">
        <p>Mauris ornare quam a lorem interdum, condimentum porta
➥ eros bibendum.</p>
    </div>

    <div class="content" id="panel3">
        <p>Cras bibendum vehicula turpis a mollis. Pellentesque
➥ tincidunt semper nunc, non porta massa volutpat quis.</p>
    </div>

    <div class="content" id="panel4">
        <p>Pellentesque accumsan tortor ut tincidunt sollicitudin.
➥</p>
    </div>

</div>
```

Straightforward, isn't it? You have to ensure that one of the `content` elements has an `active` class to help Foundation identify the initial content to display.

Don't Forget the `active` Class

If you forget to add the class `active` to one of the child elements of both `tabs` and `tabs-content` elements, then none of the tabs will be shown. You have to add the `active` class to the same positioned child element in both `tabs` and `tabs-content` elements.

This tabs component will look like Figure 4.6.

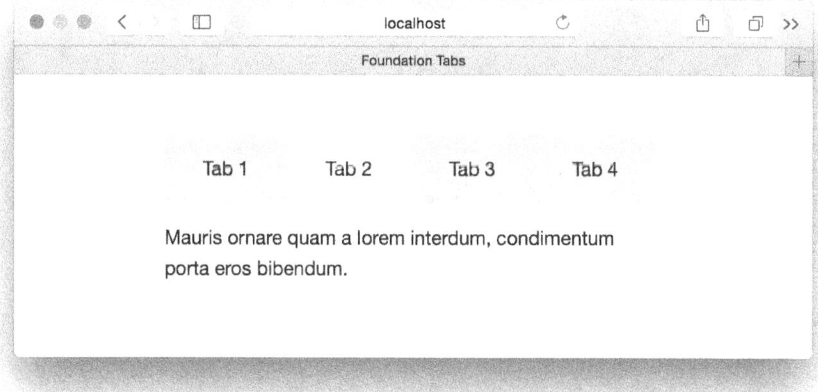

Figure 4.6. A tabs component

Foundation also lets you create an alternativeb type of the tabs component where the tabs are present on the left side and the content is present on the right side. This is called **vertical tabs**. Just insert an additional class of `vertical` and Foundation will magically convert the basic tabs component into a vertical tabs component, as shown in Figure 4.7:

```
<ul class="tabs vertical" data-tab>
   ⋮
</ul>
```

```
<div class="tabs-content">
    ⋮
</div>
```

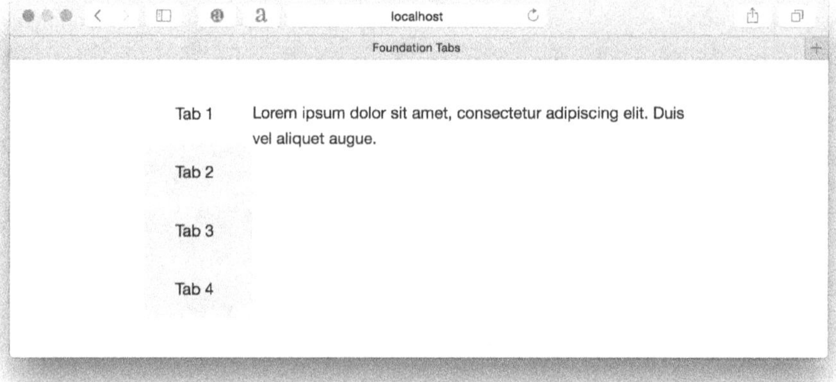

Figure 4.7. A vertical tabs component

Deep linking is a Foundation Tabs feature that gives a unique URL for each tab. For example, if your website URL is `www.mysite.com`, the URL for "tab 2" might be `www.mysite.com/#panel2`. Here `#panel2` is the ID of one of the child `content` elements in the `tabs-content` element. When a user navigates to this URL, "tab 2" will be selected by default.

To enable deep linking, pass a particular parameter to Foundation's JavaScript through the tabs component's `data-option` attribute. Here's how to do it:

```
<ul class="tabs" data-tab data-options="deep_linking: true">
  ⋮
</ul>
```

The value passed here is `deep_linking: true`. You'll find many Foundation components that come with several `data-options` parameters through which you can customize the default behaviors; check these out in the Foundation documentation.[2] We'll learn about more of them as we proceed through this book.

---

[2] http://foundation.zurb.com/docs/

Top Bar

Top bar is mainly used for navigation and other website links. Foundation's top bar component works well in all devices sizes by default (small, medium, and large screens).

To create a top bar, we need an HTML `<nav>` element with the class `top-bar`. It should also have a custom data attribute called `data-topbar` that will bind its HTML to Foundation's JavaScript:

```
<nav class="top-bar" data-topbar>
</nav>
```

This top bar will have two sections—**branding** and **content**. Branding is where the website's title or logo goes. Content contains all the links and drop-down menus that you want in the navigation bar. Let's see how to create them.

The branding section is created using an unordered list `<ul>` with the class `title-area` . It has an `<li>` element with a class `name` that contains the title of the website:

```
<nav class="top-bar" data-topbar>
    <ul class="title-area">
        <li class="name">
            <h1><a href="#">My Site</a></h1>
        </li>
    </ul>
</nav>
```

The navigation bar should look like Figure 4.8.

Figure 4.8. The branding section on our top bar

Let's add a hamburger icon that will be visible only when the browser width is too small to display the complete navigation bar. This icon goes inside the `title-area` element:

top-bar.html *(excerpt)*

```
<nav class="top-bar" data-topbar>
    <ul class="title-area">
        <li class="name">
            <h1><a href="#">My Site</a></h1>
        </li>

        <!-- Hamburger icon -->
        <li class="toggle-topbar menu-icon"><a href="#"><span>Menu
➥</span></a></li>

    </ul>
</nav>
```

The hamburger icon should have the classes `toggle-topbar` and `menu-icon`. The first class binds the click operation on the top bar, and the second class is used to add CSS styling. It also has a `<span>` element with the text "Menu." Now when the browser width is too small, we'll see the icon as shown in Figure 4.9.

Figure 4.9. Our top bar component on a smaller screen, diplaying the hamburger icon

Next we have the main content section of the navigation bar. This is defined using HTML's `<section>` element with a class of `top-bar-section`. This section is divided into two categories of links: right-side links and left-side links. Let's check them out:

```
<section class="top-bar-section">
    <ul class="right">
        ⋮
    </ul>
    <ul class="left">
        ⋮
    </ul>
</section>
```

Both left- and right-side links are defined using the `<ul>` elements. The right-side elements have a class of `right` while the left-side elements have a class of `left`. Now you can insert as many links using `<li>` and `<a>` elements inside them. Here's the final markup for the top bar:

top-bar.html *(excerpt)*

```
<nav class="top-bar" data-topbar>
    <ul class="title-area">
        <li class="name">
            <h1><a href="#">My Site</a></h1>
        </li>
        <li class="toggle-topbar menu-icon"><a href="#"><span>Menu
➥</span></a></li>
    </ul>

    <section class="top-bar-section">
      <ul class="left">
          <li class="active"><a href="#">Home</a></li>
          <li><a href="#">Products</a></li>
          <li><a href="#">Services</a></li>
          <li><a href="#">Consulting</a></li>
      </ul>
      <ul class="right">
          <li><a href="#">Our team</a></li>
          <li><a href="#">Contact us</a></li>
          <li><a href="#">About us</a></li>
      </ul>

   </section>
</nav>
```

Figure 4.10 shows how the top bar looks in larger screens.

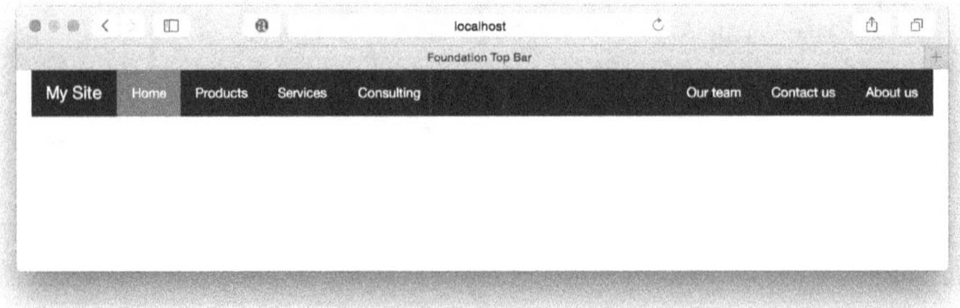

Figure 4.10. Our navigation on larger screens

Figure 4.11 shows how the top bar looks when the hamburger icon is tapped on mobile devices.

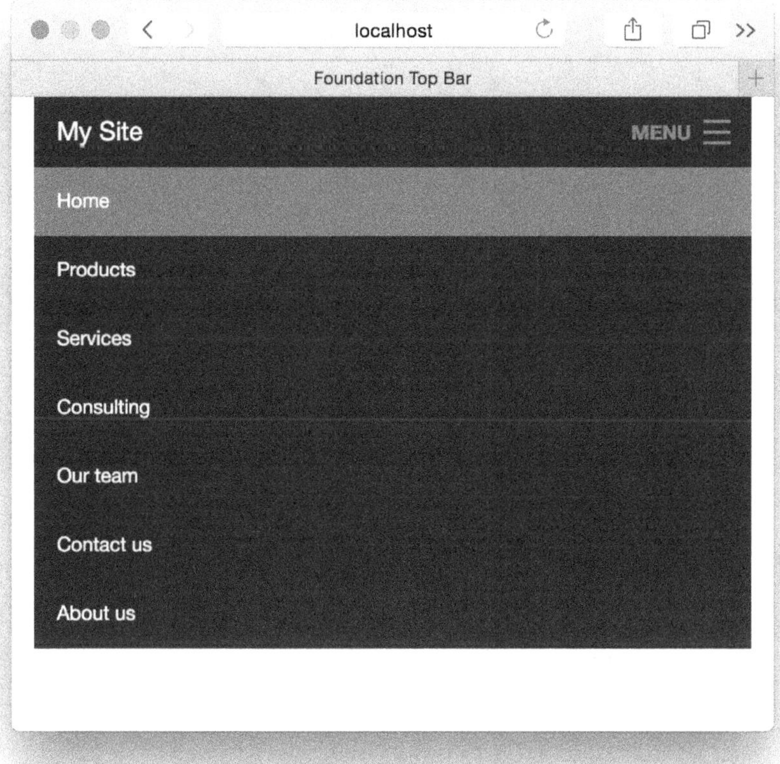

Figure 4.11. Our navigation on smaller screens

Amazing, isn't it? We didn't have to write a single line of JavaScript code to make a working, responsive navigation bar. That's the beauty of using the Foundation framework.

Let's add a drop-down menu in this navigation bar. First we'll add a special class `has-dropdown` to the `<li>` element with the nested links. Then we add an anchor tag `<a>` along with a nested unordered list `<ul>` inside the `has-dropdown` element:

top-bar.html *(excerpt)*

```
<li class="has-dropdown">
        <a href="#">Our network</a>
        <ul class="dropdown">
```

```
                <li><a href="#">Learnable</a></li>
                <li><a href="#">SitePoint</a></li>
        </ul>
</li>
```

You should have a similar result to Figure 4.12.

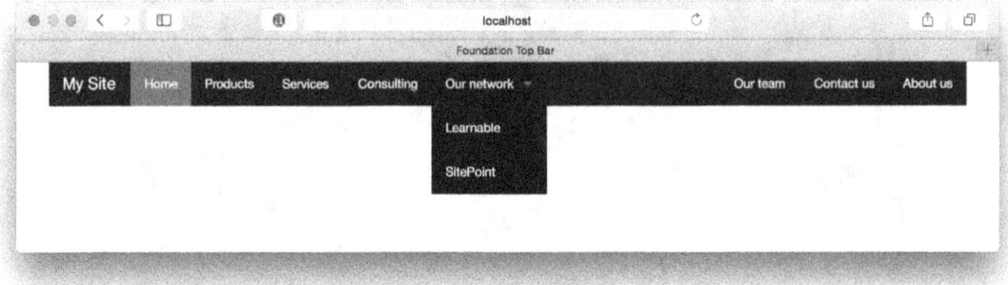

Figure 4.12. The drop-down menu

The menu is responsive. When collapsed onto smaller screens, it appears sideways with an arrow icon indication, as seen in Figure 4.13.

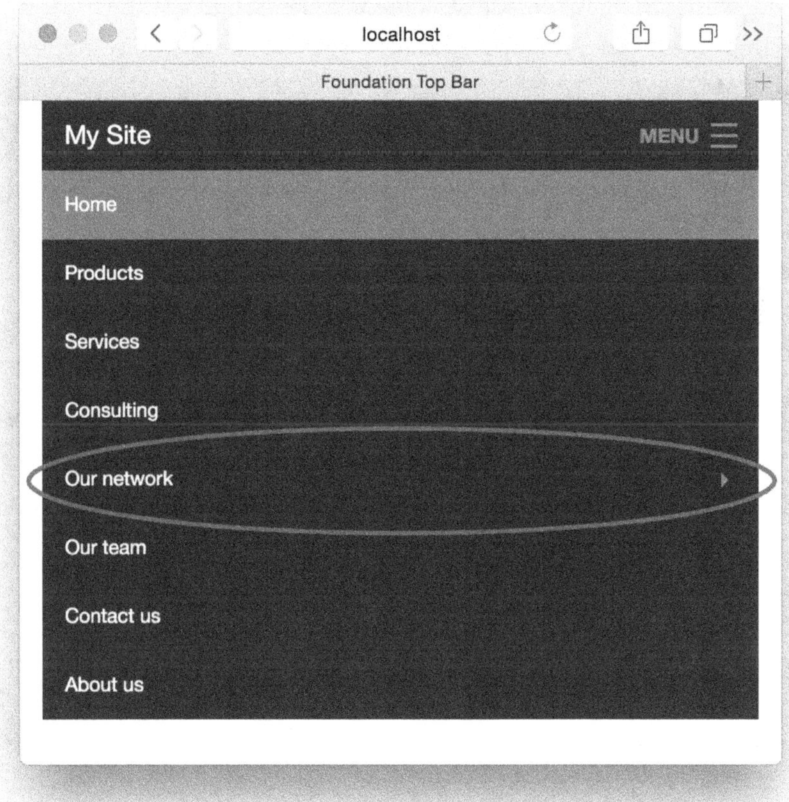

Figure 4.13. The drop-down menu on a smaller screen

There are a few additional useful and interesting things that you can do with the top bar component:

- **Fixed top bar**: For the top bar to stay fixed as you scroll, wrap the whole `<nav>` element inside a `<div>` element with the class `fixed`. The top bar takes the width of the browser window and stays fixed to the window's ceiling.
- **Contain to grid**: By default, the top bar takes the browser width. If you want your navigation to be set to your grid width, wrap it in a `<div>` element with the class `contain-to-grid`.

- **Sticky top bar**: Suppose you have a navigation bar in the middle of the web page and you want it to float and stick to the top when it touches the browser ceiling. This can be achieved by wrapping the navigation bar in a `<div>` element with the class `sticky`.

- **Respond to click**: By default, the drop-down menu in th top bar component responds to the mouse hover. You can override this functionality and make it respond to the mouse click instead by passing a parameter `is_hover: false` to the `data-option` attribute.

  For example:

```
<nav class="top-bar" data-topbar data-options="is_hover: false">
  ⋮
</nav>
```

Summary

Throughout this chapter, we learned how to create and organize the content of our website. First we saw how to create Foundation panels, alerts, and tables. We took a step further and made the table responsive by placing an additional stylesheet to our project. Then we proceeded to create intuitive tabs and saw how to make these vertical by adding just a single class. Finally, we learned how to create amazing top bars (navigation bars) and add a drop-down menu to it.

In the next chapter, we'll check out how to manage and organize pictures and videos by creating sliders and thumbnails.

Chapter 5

Handling Media

In this chapter, we're going to learn some ways to to add snazzy videos and images to our sites using Foundation and then add some styling. We'll discover some handy components that add to the user experience, such as image slideshows and lightboxes. So, let's take a look.

Integrating Video into Your Page

What do you do when you need to integrate a YouTube video into your web page? You grab the HTML embed code from YouTube and paste it into your HTML file, right? However, these embed codes usually come with a predefined height and width, so making such videos responsive can be difficult.

Fortunately, Foundation gives us a component called **flex video** that wraps the embed code of any video source and makes it responsive. Creating a flex video is extremely easy. You just have to add the class `flex-video` to the `<div>` element and you're done. Here's an example of flex video that contains a YouTube embed code:

```
<div class="flex-video">
      <iframe width="420" height="315" src="//www.youtube.com/
➥embed/k85mRPqvMbE" frameborder="0" allowfullscreen></iframe>
</div>
```

Note that this YouTube embed code comes with a height and a width attribute hardcoded from YouTube. Yet Foundation's flex video component will just ignore them and make the video fit the parent grid container.

Using Foundation, let's create a grid system with a centered central column that's six virtual columns wide on large screens and eight virtual columns wide on small screens. Then we'll insert a flex video component into it:

flex-video.html *(excerpt)*

```
<div class="large-6 large-offset-3 small-8 small-offset-2 columns">
    <div class="flex-video">
        <iframe width="420" height="315" src="//www.youtube.com/
➥embed/k85mRPqvMbE" frameborder="0" allowfullscreen></iframe>
    </div>
</div>
```

You should see a similar sight to Figure 5.1 in your browser.

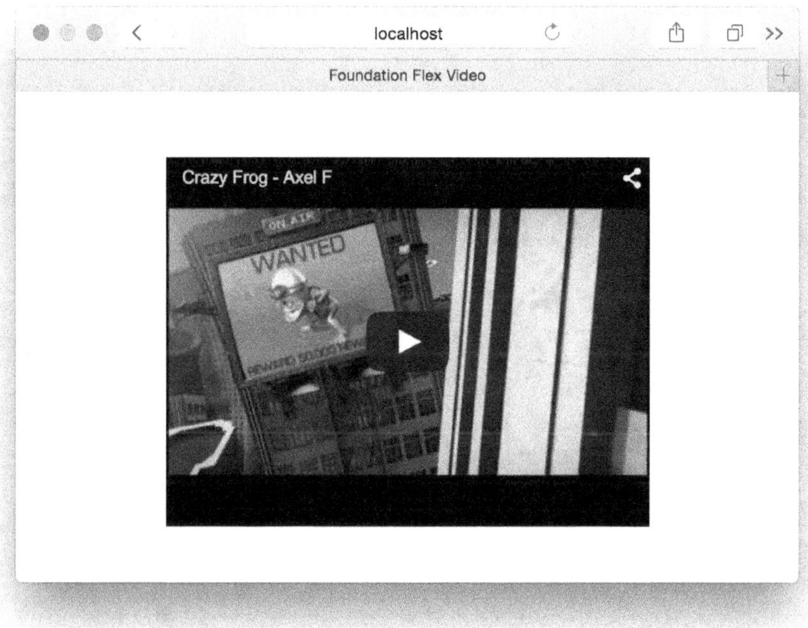

Figure 5.1. A flex video component

Now if you try to resize the browser width, you'll see that the width of the video also changes. It takes the full width of the centered grid column.

Foundation provides two additional CSS classes for styling flex video: `widescreen` and `vimeo`. Normally, embedded videos are square in shape. If you want to make it look wider or rectangular, add the class `widescreen` to the `flex-video` element. This will add a `padding-bottom` of `56.34%` to the flex video. The class `vimeo` can also be added to the flex video when Vimeo videos are embedded. This removes extra padding from embedded Vimeo videos.

Creating a Responsive Image Slideshow

I can still remember the huge amount of CSS and JavaScript code I had to write to create my first image slideshow. Well, things are much simpler now, thanks to Foundation's image slideshow component called **Orbit**.

A basic Orbit component is created using a single unordered list `<ul>` tag with the `data-orbit` attribute:

```
<ul data-orbit>
</ul>
```

Every `<li>` tag inside this list will represent a slide in your slideshow, with each `<li>` element containing an `<img>` tag; for example:

```
<ul data-orbit>
    <li>
        <img src="[path to image 1]"/>
    </li>
    <li>
        <img src="[path to image 1]"/>
    </li>
</ul>
```

If you try this out, you'll see a fully fledged image slideshow in your browser, as shown in Figure 5.2.

Figure 5.2. An example of the Orbit image slider

Looks great, doesn't it? Let's add some more features to this slider.

For captions, add a <div> element with the class `orbit-caption` in each <li> element:

orbit.html *(excerpt)*

```
<ul data-orbit>
    <li>
        <img src="[path to image 1]"/>
        <div class="orbit-caption">
            First slide caption. Lorem ipsum dolor sit amet,
➥ consectetur adipiscing elit.
        </div>
    </li>
    <li>
        <img src="[path to image 1]"/>
        <div class="orbit-caption">
            Second slide caption. Lorem ipsum dolor sit amet,
➥ consectetur adipiscing elit.
        </div>
    </li>
</ul>
```

If you refresh the browser, you'll see text appearing below each image, as shown in Figure 5.3.

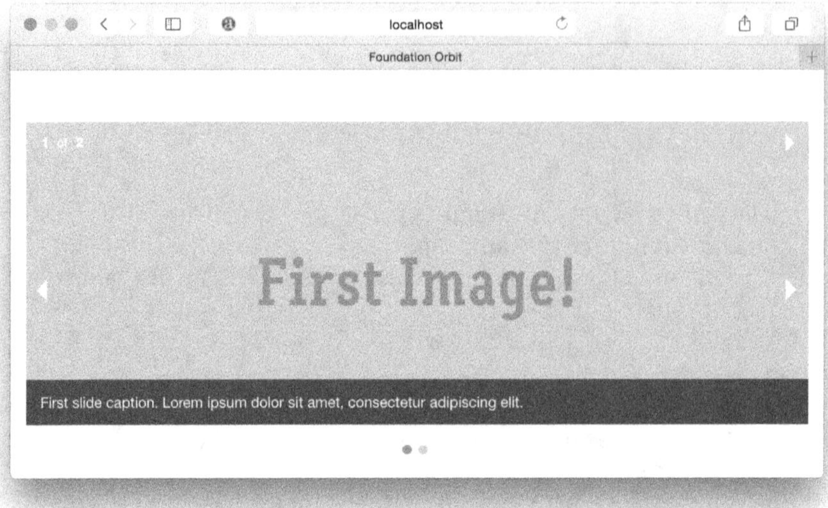

Figure 5.3. Captions added to our slideshow

Foundation's Orbit component is responsive by default but also responds to mobile touch gestures. If you swipe left or right on mobile devices, the slides will change accordingly.

Orbit is Marked for Deprecation

Foundation's Orbit component has been marked for deprecation. While it's still included in the Foundation package, it's likely that it will be removed in the future. We've included it here because it's still a useful way to easily add a slideshow to your page, and it's included with the Foundation package by default. Alternative third-party slideshow components, such as Slick Carousel[1], can also be used to add image slideshows to your page instead. In the next section, we'll discuss the Clearing component, which provides an alternative way to present images that's included in the default Foundation pachage.

[1] http://kenwheeler.github.io/slick/

Creating Image Lightboxes with the Clearing Component

While making slideshows using Orbit is easy, it can be unsuitable for creating certain image slideshows. One of the major problems of Orbit is its inability to handle variable height images.

With the **Clearing** component, it's possible to create an image slideshow that displays images in full-screen mode and handles variable height images properly. It looks similar to the photo lightbox of Google+, showing a set of small image thumbnails that when clicked display the image full screen. Let's check out how to create a Clearing component:

clearing.html *(excerpt)*

```
<ul class="clearing-thumbs" data-clearing>
  <li><a href="path/to/your/img"><img src="path/to/your/img-th"></a>
➥</li>
  <li><a href="path/to/your/img"><img src="path/to/your/img-th"></a>
➥</li>
  <li><a href="path/to/your/img"><img src="path/to/your/img-th"></a>
➥</li>
</ul>
```

As you can see, you need to set up an unordered list with the class `.clearing-thumbs` and add the `data-clearing` attribute. Every `<li>` element in the list represents a thumbnail image containing an anchor tag that wraps an image tag. The anchor tag links to the original image while the image tag contains the path to the image thumbnail.

The only disadvantage in opting for the Clearing component over an Orbit component is that you have to create two different image sizes—thumbnail and full-size image—for each image that you include.

The Clearing component we created will look like Figure 5.4.

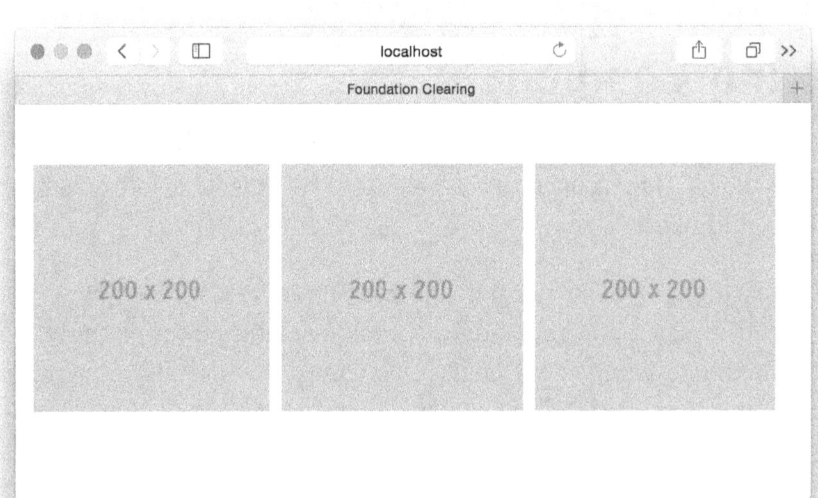

Figure 5.4. An example of a Clearing component

When you click on any of these thumbnails, you'll have the full-size image shown in a lightbox as shown in Figure 5.5.

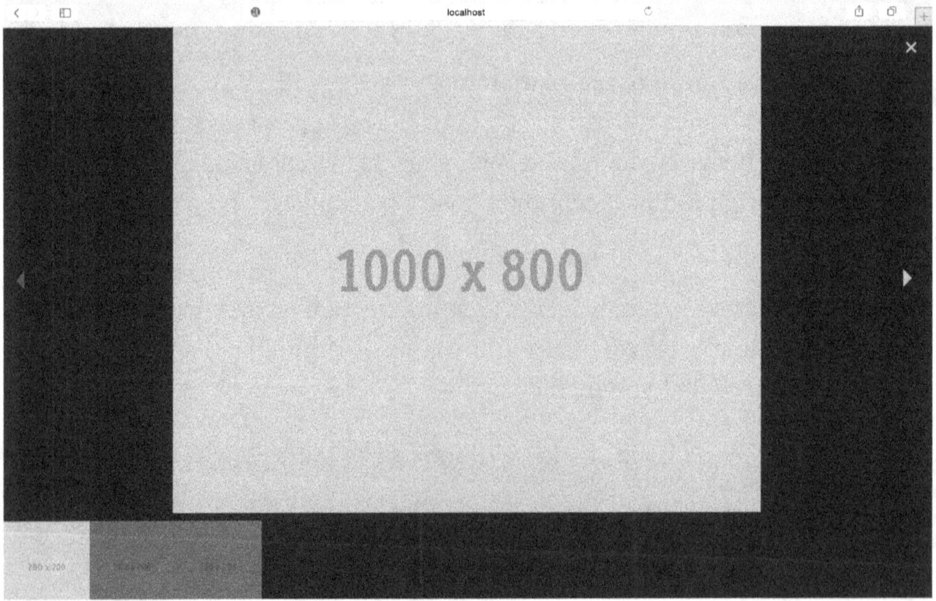

Figure 5.5. After clicking a thumbnail, the full-size image is shown.

If you want to style the thumbnails, add the class `th` to every `<li>` element in the list:

clearing.html *(excerpt)*

```
<ul class="clearing-thumbs" data-clearing>
  <li class="th"><a href="path/to/your/img"><img src="path/to/your/
➥img-th"></a></li>
  ⋮
</ul>
```

Now every thumbnail image has a border with some padding, making them look more like thumbnails.

For an image caption, add the `data-caption` attribute with your caption text as the value to the image tag:

clearing.html *(excerpt)*

```
<ul class="clearing-thumbs" data-clearing>
  <li class="th"><a href="path/to/your/img"><img src="path/to/your/
➥img-th" data-caption="First image caption"></a></li>
  ⋮
</ul>
```

Summary

In this chapter, we've handled two important types of media—videos and images—using various components in Foundation. First, we saw how to create responsive images using flex videos. Then we saw how to create a beautiful image slideshow using the Orbit component. Finally, we learned about the Clearing component, one of the best ways to display images in any website.

In the next chapter, we'll learn how easy it is to create and style forms in Foundation. We'll also see how to create intuitive switch buttons and range sliders, and talk about client-side form validations in Foundation through the Abide validation library.

Chapter 6

Working With Forms

Forms are a crucial component of any website. Sign-in pages, registration pages, comment boxes, feedback sections and surveys are all HTML forms. While using basic HTML markup to create forms is easy, styling every form element can be a tedious task.

In this chapter, we'll learn how to create beautiful, responsive forms using the Foundation framework. We'll explore Foundation's form validation classes, and how to validate our forms with Abide. Finally, we'll discover how to use the Foundation toggle switches such as the on/off buttons in iOS devices. Finally, we'll explore Foundation's form validation classes. So, let's get started.

Building a Basic Form

Unlike many other front-end frameworks, such as Bootstrap, Foundation provides no specific CSS classes for HTML forms. Foundation's main CSS file includes default styles for every basic HTML element. As always, if you want to override a style or use a new style, you are free to do it in your **app.css** file.

The Foundation grid system is used in forms to control the width of the form's input elements, as well as to place the form elements at the right place. Let's examine how to place two different HTML input elements side by side in Foundation:

```
<form>
    <div class="row">
        <div class="small-6 columns">
            <input type="text" placeholder="First Name" />
        </div>
        <div class="small-6 columns">
            <input type="text" placeholder="Last Name"/>
        </div>
    </div>
</form>
```

Here we have two different columns using the classes `small-6` and `columns`. An input element has been placed into each column that takes the width of each of the columns. This form appears in Figure 6.1.

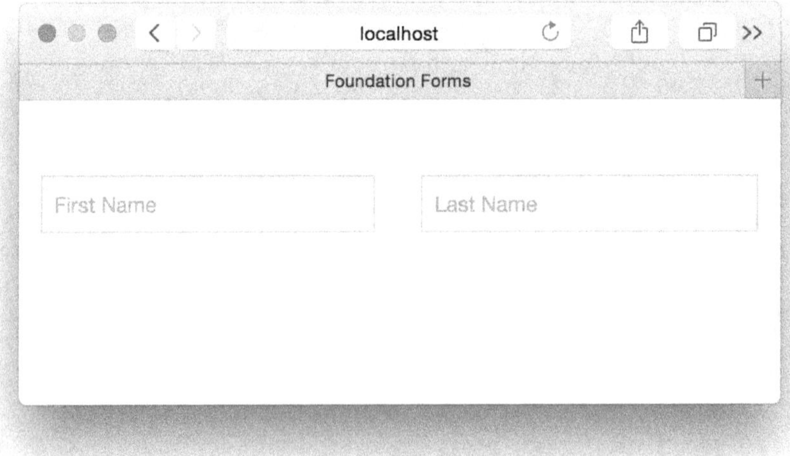

Figure 6.1. A basic form layout

To add a label to an input tag, wrap a `<label>` tag around the `<input/>` tag as follows:

```
<label>First Name
    <input type="text" placeholder="First Name" />
</label>
```

Wrapping a label around the input element associates it with the corresponding input element. If wrapping a `<label>` tag around the form is not suitable for your application, you can use the `for` attribute on the `<label>` tag. The `for` attribute should have the ID of the `<input>` element.

Figure 6.1 will look like Figure 6.2 after adding a label to each input tag.

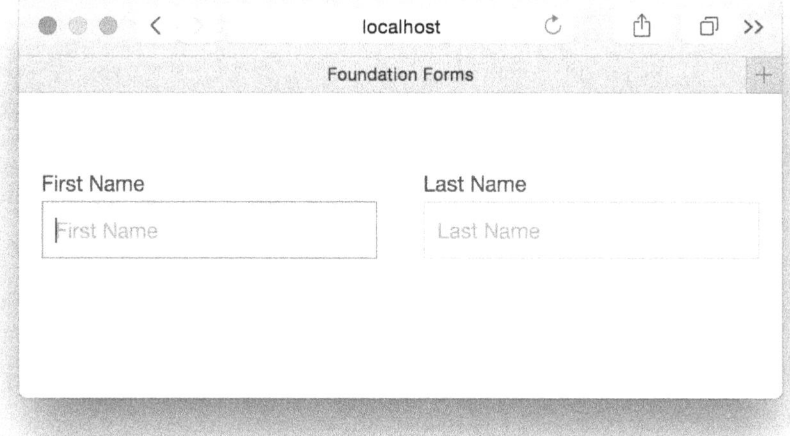

Figure 6.2. Our form with labels added

You can also wrap `<select>` and `<textarea>` elements with labels. Let's add `<select>` and `<textarea>` elements to our existing form:

index.html *(excerpt)*

```
<form>
    <div class="row">
        <div class="small-6 columns">
            <input type="text" placeholder="First Name" />
        </div>
        <div class="small-6 columns">
            <input type="text" placeholder="Last Name"/>
```

```
        </div>
    </div>
    <div class="row">
        <div class="large-12 columns">
            <label>Select Place
                <select>
                    <option value="husker">Alabama</option>
                    <option value="starbuck">Alaska</option>
                    <option value="hotdog">Arizona</option>
                    <option value="apollo">California</option>
                </select>
            </label>
        </div>
    </div>
    <div class="row">
        <div class="large-12 columns">
            <label>Add comment
                <textarea placeholder="Write something"></textarea>
            </label>
        </div>
    </div>
</form>
```

The form now should look as Figure 6.3 does.

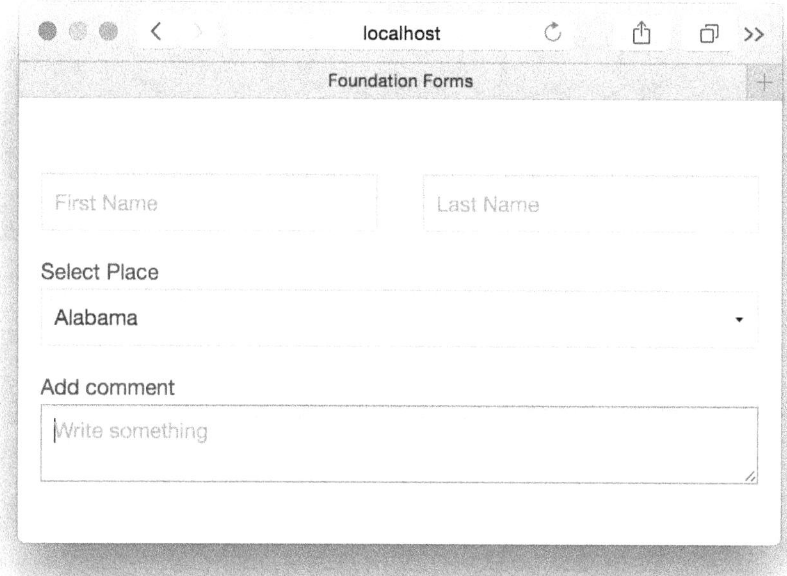

Figure 6.3. Our form with <select> and <textarea> elements added.

Now let's add some radio buttons and checkboxes to our example form:

index.html *(excerpt)*

```
<div class="row">
    <div class="large-6 columns">
        <label>Select Gender</label>
        <input type="radio" name="gender" value="male" id="
➥maleRadio"><label for="maleRadio">Male</label>
        <input type="radio" name="gender" value="female" id="
➥femaleRadio"><label for="femaleRadio">Female</label>
    </div>

    <div class="large-6 columns">
        <label>Preferred Color</label>
        <input id="blueCheckbox" type="checkbox"><label for="
➥blueCheckbox">Blue</label>
        <input id="redCheckbox" type="checkbox"><label for="
```

```
➥redCheckbox">Red</label>
    </div>
</div>
```

The result should be similar to Figure 6.4.

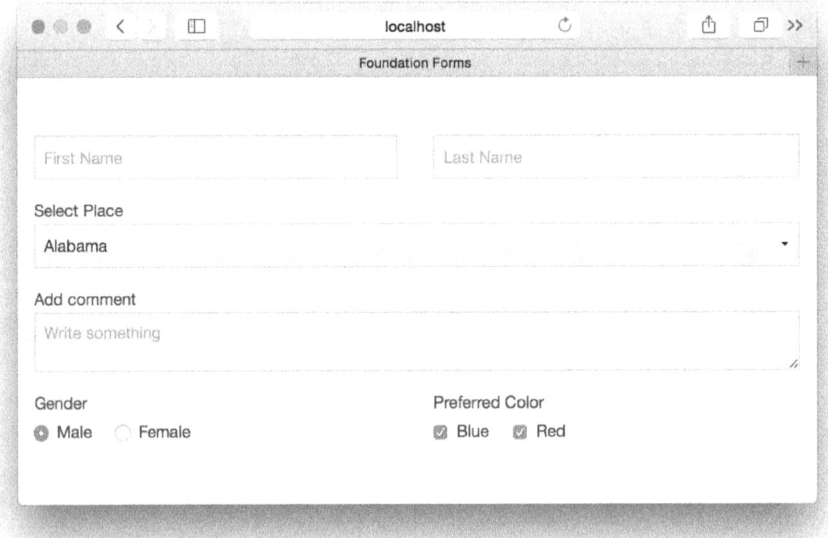

Figure 6.4. Our example form evolves with radio buttons and checkboxes added.

Prefix and Postfix Input Fields

Foundation has two types of input fields: prefix (in which symbols such as $ and € can be added) and postfix (where text such as '.com' can be added). This can be seen in Figure 6.5.

Figure 6.5. Prefix and postfix input fields.

To create a prefix or postfix input field, first build a two-column layout using the Foundation grid system. Then produce a `<div>` element with the classes `row` and `collapse`. Here, `collapse` will help in removing the default padding and margin between columns:

```
<div class="row collapse">
</div>
```

Next, we add columns inside this `row` element. To create a prefix input box, construct a thin column and then a wide column. Let's select `small-3` for the thin column and `small-9` for the wide column:

```
<div class="row collapse">
  <div class="small-3 columns">
  </div>
  <div class="small-9 columns">
  </div>
</div>
```

Remember to add the class `columns` or `column` along with the column widths. Add your desired prefix text, such as '$', with the help of a `<span>` tag inside the thin column. It should have the class `prefix` to apply the CSS style:

```
<div class="small-3 columns">
    <span class="prefix">$</span>
</div>
```

Now add the input field inside the wide column:

```
<div class="small-9 columns">
    <input type="text" placeholder="Enter Amount"/>
</div>
```

Try checking this code in the browser. You should have a prefix input box indicating that you should enter a dollar amount.

For a postfix input box, simply exchange the positions of the thin and wide columns. Then use the class `postfix` for the `<span>` tag instead of `prefix`. Here's the code for a postfix input box:

```
<div class="row collapse">
    <div class="small-9 columns">
        <input type="text" placeholder="example" />
    </div>
    <div class="small-3 columns">
        <span class="postfix">.com</span>
    </div>
</div>
```

Inlining Label and Input Fields

Sometimes you may need to place the label left of the input field instead of on top of it. You can do this with the help of the grid system and some additional CSS classes.

We have to create two columns, one thin and one wide. We'll use the class `small-3` for the thin column and `small-9` for the wide column:

```
<div class="row collapse">
    <div class="small-3 columns">
    </div>
    <div class="small-9 columns">
    </div>
</div>
```

Add a `<label>` tag to the thin column as follows:

```
<div class="small-3 columns">
    <label for="nameField">Enter Name</label>
</div>
```

Now place an input field in the wide column:

```
<div class="small-9 columns">
    <input type="text" id="nameField" placeholder="John Doe" />
</div>
```

Let's check it out on the browser. It will look like Figure 6.6.

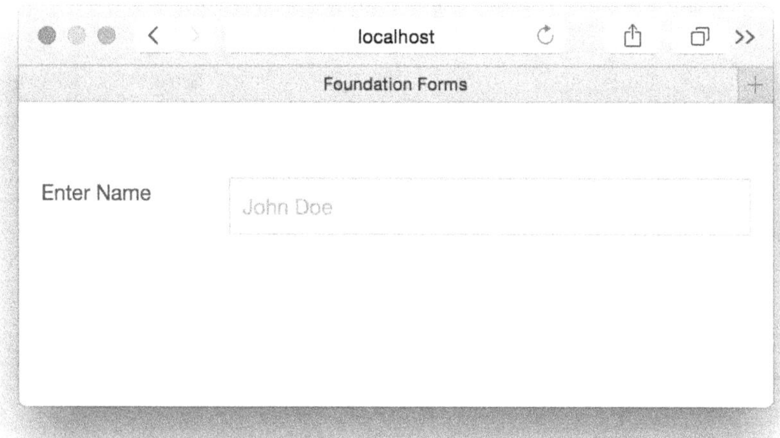

Figure 6.6. An inline label

There's a small issue here, however. The label looks vertically misaligned with respect to the input box. We need to add some CSS classes to make it look perfect. Adding the class `right` to the label text will make it float right. This will bring it closer to the input field. Adding another CSS class `inline` will add some padding and margin to it.

```
<div class="small-3 columns">
    <label for="nameField" class="right inline">Enter Name</label>
</div>
```

If you reload the browser page, you should see a perfectly aligned label text as shown in Figure 6.7.

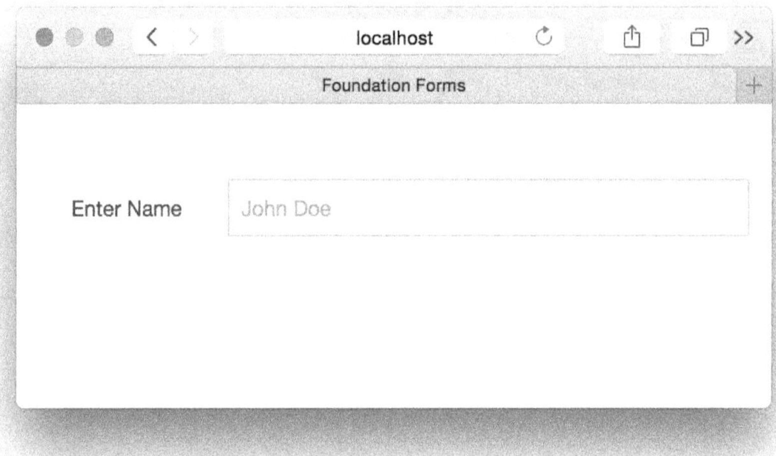

Figure 6.7. Our adjusted inline label

Error States

Indicating whether an input field has an invalid entry is extremely straightforward in Foundation. Simply add the class `error` to the label text to make it red. You can also place additional text below the input field for an error message. This text is added using a `<small>` tag with a class `error`. Here's an example of an input field with an error state:

index.html *(excerpt)*

```
<div class="small-12 columns">
    <label class="error">Name
        <input type="text" placeholder="Name" />
    </label>
    <small class="error">Invalid entry</small>
</div>
```

This will look similar to Figure 6.8.

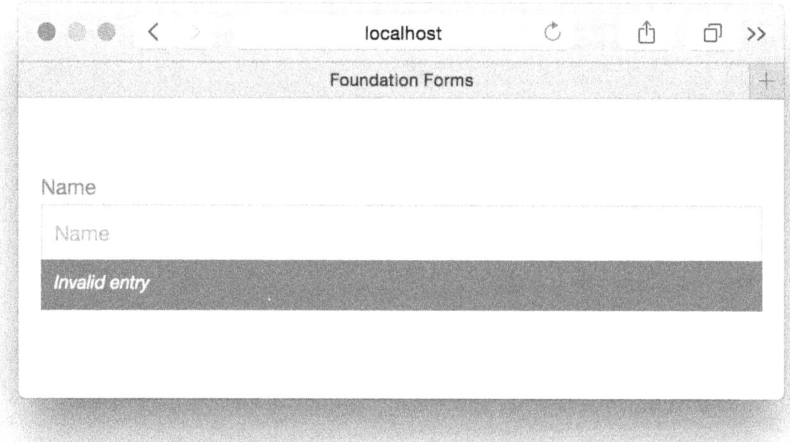

Figure 6.8. Indicating an error state on the form

Note that we've yet to actually carry out any validation of the form here. A simple way to do this is to use the Abide validation library, which we'll cover next.

Validating Forms Using Abide

Abide is a library that Foundation supports to provide client-side form validation, and comes preloaded in Foundation's complete package. In the previous section, we saw how to *indicate* an error state in a form but we're yet to learn when and how to *invoke* those error states. We'll now use Abide to add client-side validation to our form.

Here's a demo form that we'll use:

```
<form>
  <div class="name-field">
    <label>Your name
      <input type="text"/>
    </label>
    <small class="error">Name is required and must be a string.
➥</small>
  </div>
  <div class="email-field">
    <label>Email
```

```
      <input type="email"/>
    </label>
    <small class="error">An email address is required.</small>
  </div>
  <button type="submit">Submit</button>
</form>
```

This basic form asks for the name and email address of the user, and will look like the form in Figure 6.9.

Your name

Name is required and must be a string.

Email

An email address is required.

Submit

Figure 6.9. Our form without validation

The error states are visible up-front because we're yet to set up Abide validation. To do so, we include an additional JavaScript file into our **index.html** file. This file is called **foundation.abide.js** and is present inside the **js/foundation/** folder of your project. Place this file at the bottom of the **index.html** file, just below the Foundation JavaScript line as follows:

```
⋮
<script src="js/vendor/jquery.js"></script>
<script src="js/foundation.min.js"></script>
<script src="js/foundation/foundation.abide.js"></script>
⋮
```

Next, we initialize the Abide library on our form by adding the attribute `data-abide` to the `<form>` tag:

```
<form data-abide>
  ⋮
</form>
```

The error states should now be hidden after you reload the page, as shown in Figure 6.10.

Your name

Email

Submit

Figure 6.10. The form with error states hidden by Abide

If you submit this form, you'll see that the validation fails to work. This is because we haven't told Abide library which fields to validate. The most basic validation requirement is for the form fields not being empty. We'll use HTML5's `required` attribute to add the necessary validation to the form input fields:

index.html *(excerpt)*

```
<form data-abide>
  <div class="name-field">
    <label>Your name
      <input type="text" required/>
    </label>
    <small class="error">Name is required and must be a string.
➥</small>
  </div>
  <div class="email-field">
    <label>Email
      <input type="email" required/>
    </label>
    <small class="error">An email address is required.</small>
  </div>
  <button type="submit">Submit</button>
</form>
```

Now if you try to submit the form—after reloading the page, of course—you'll see that validation is working and empty fields aren't accepted, as shown in Figure 6.11.

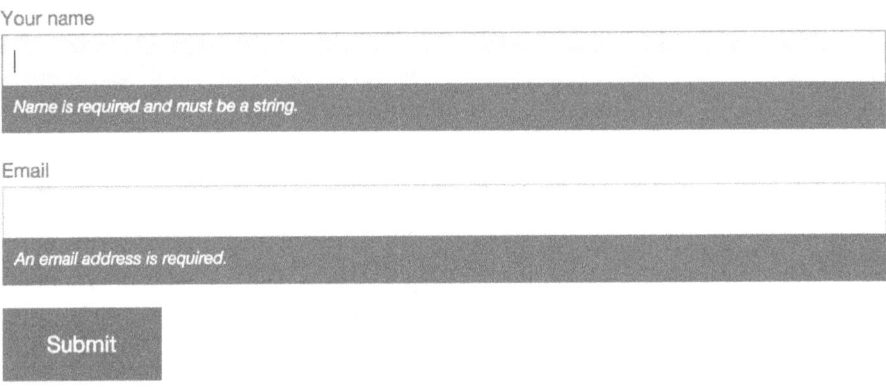

Figure 6.11. The form now rejects empty fields

We'll refine our form validation by adding more details. Abide validation enables you add patterns to each input field so that it will accept only particular values. For example, if you want the name fields to accept only characters and exclude numbers, there's a specific pattern that you must supply to the Abide library. The patterns are also known as **regular expressions** or **RegEx**. You can read more about RegEx on the Mozilla Developer Network.[1] Another cool online tool that lets you grab a pattern easily is HTML5Pattern.[2] You can also refer to Foundation's documentation for some predefined patterns.[3]

Let's add the pattern `[a-zA-Z]+` to the name field. This will force just alphabetical characters to be submitted:

```
<input type="text" required pattern="[a-zA-Z]+"/>
```

If you now try to submit the form with an invalid entry, such as numbers, you'll receive an error in the name field.

---

[1] https://developer.mozilla.org/en/docs/Web/JavaScript/Guide/Regular_Expressions
[2] https://html5pattern.com
[3] http://foundation.zurb.com/docs/components/abide.html#predefined-patterns

One-sided Error Checking

The Abide validation library provides client-side validation only. It checks for errors on the browser using JavaScript, so if JavaScript is disabled on the user's browser, it will fail to work. We recommend that you always validate forms on the server side as well, using a programming language such as PHP or Ruby.

Switches

Switches are a toggle element that change between an on-and-off state on tap or click, as shown in Figure 6.12.

Figure 6.12. A switch

What's best about the switches in the Foundation framework is that they're made using regular checkbox and radio button HTML elements. Hence, you can use traditional JavaScript methods to detect the state of these elements.

To create a switch, set up a `<div>` element with the class `switch`. Then insert an HTML checkbox with label markup inside of it:

```
<div class="switch">
  <input id="exampleCheckboxSwitch" type="checkbox">
  <label for="exampleCheckboxSwitch"></label>
</div>
```

You need to ensure that the `for` attribute of the label element contains the ID value of the input checkbox element.

Figure 6.13 shows how this should look.

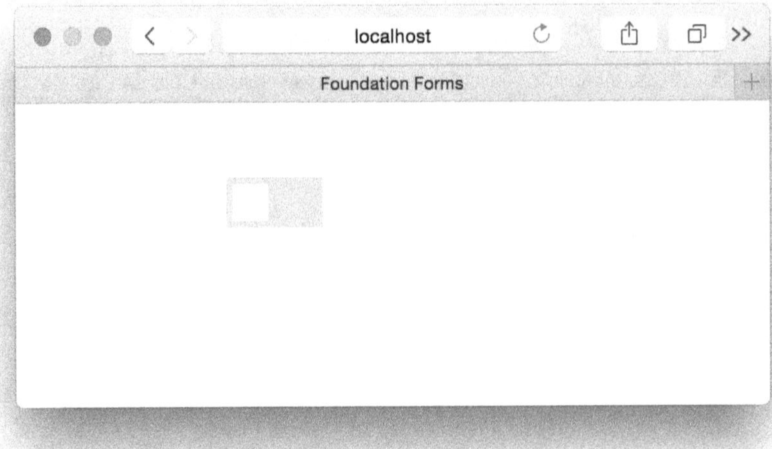

Figure 6.13. A basic toggle switch

You can also create a set of radio button switches using the same markup. Make sure you give all the switches the same `name` attribute, as shown in the code. With radio-button-powered switches, you ensure that only one switch at a time can be selected:

```
<div class="switch">
  <input id="exampleRadioSwitch1" type="radio" checked name="
➥testGroup">
  <label for="exampleRadioSwitch1"></label>
</div>

<div class="switch">
  <input id="exampleRadioSwitch2" type="radio" name="testGroup">
  <label for="exampleRadioSwitch2"></label>
</div>

<div class="switch">
  <input id="exampleRadioSwitch3" type="radio" name="testGroup">
  <label for="exampleRadioSwitch3"></label>
</div>
```

The result will look like Figure 6.14.

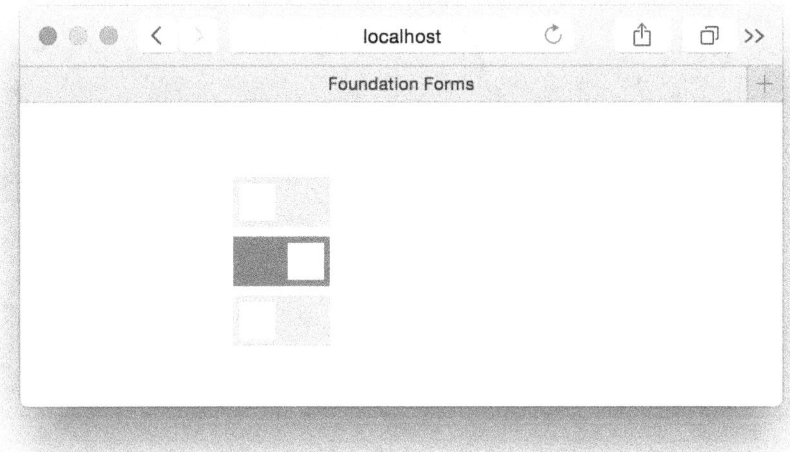

Figure 6.14. Radio-button-powered switches

Sizing Switches

You can also control the shape and size of switches using a few CSS classes:

- `large`: for a larger switch
- `small`: for a smaller switch
- `tiny`: for an extra small switch

You can also add the following classes to change the shape of your switches:

- `radius`: adds a border radius of `4px`
- `round`: adds a border radius of `2rem`

Here's an example of these classes in use:

```
<div class="switch large radius">
  <input id="exampleRadioSwitch4" type="radio" name="testGroup">
  <label for="exampleRadioSwitch4"></label>
</div>
```

This will create a large switch with a border radius of `4px`.

Figure 6.15 shows all the shapes and sizes of switches.

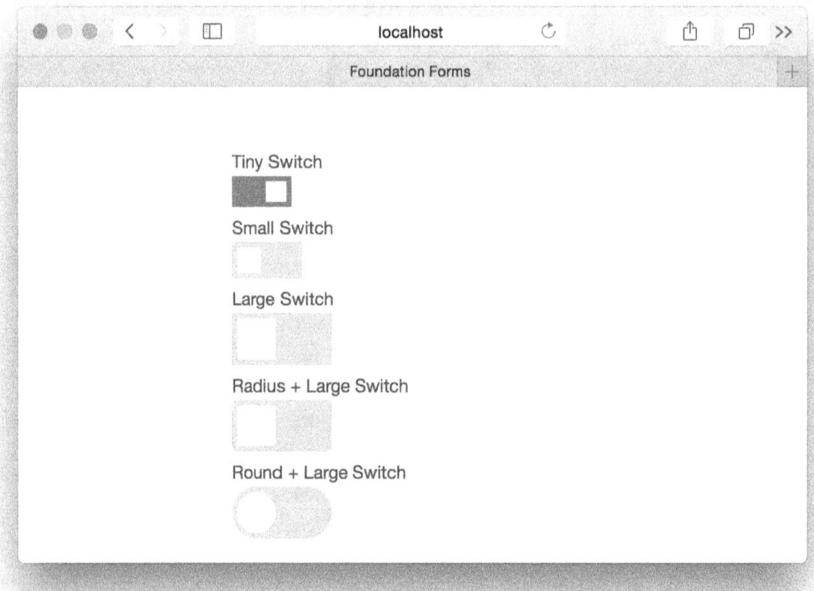

Figure 6.15. A smorgasbord of switch sizes and styling

Disabling Switch

There may be cases where you'll want to disable switches so that they cannot be selected. The easiest way to do this is to use HTML5's default `disabled` attribute. It can be added to any HTML tag so that the click event will fail on that tag. By default, Foundation provides no classes for styling checkbox and radio switches with the `disabled` attribute set.

However, if you add the `disabled` attribute to the switch markup in the previous section, you'll find that the switch's toggling animation still works; however, the checkbox or radio button won't actually be functional in the background. We need to fix this by writing our own CSS styles for the disabled state of the switch.

Add the following CSS code to your custom CSS file:

```
.switch.disabled {
  opacity: 0.25;
  pointer-events: none; // Prevents click events from working
}
```

Then add the class `disabled` to the `switch` element, and the attribute `disabled` to the `<input>` element; for example:

```
<div class="switch large round disabled">
  <input id="exampleSwitch" type="radio" disabled="" name="
➥testGroup">
  <label for="exampleSwitch"></label>
</div>
```

You should see a similar sight to Figure 6.16.

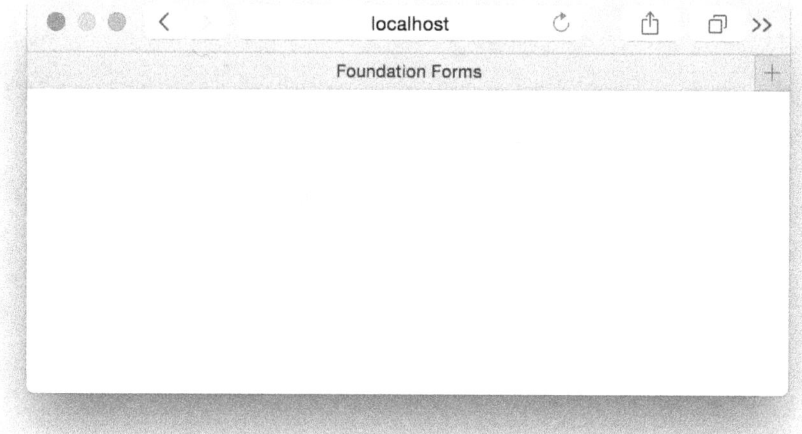

Figure 6.16. A disabled switch

Summary

I trust you had fun learning about forms in Foundation. In this chapter, we learned that the secret to creating beautiful forms is all about mastering Foundation's grid system and adding a few CSS classes. We also explored how to create prefix and postfix input fields and how to inline labels with respect to input fields, and how to indicate errors and validate our forms. Finally, we saw how to build an intuitive switches element.

In the next chapter, we'll discover how to customize Foundation's default CSS styles using the Sass CSS preprocessor. So take a quick break, and then buckle yourself in for this exciting final chapter of this book.

Chapter 7

Customizing Foundation Using Sass

One of the major problems with CSS frameworks is that the component design can become al-too common on websites as more developers start using the framework, making websites look very, well, same-y. Those in the know can easily identify whether a website is using a particular framework. This is why it's important to customize our frameworks. The more customization support a framework provides, the easier it is for developers to make changes to the base design.

Foundation's CSS was created using **Sass.** Now you might be wondering just what the heck Sass is? Well, it's a CSS **preprocessor** that brings dynamic components such as variables to CSS. As the name suggests, it preprocesses these dynamic CSS files into static CSS files that will be used in the websites you create. We'll understand it better by looking at an example. Imagine you have selected a particular shade of blue and used it at various places in your stylesheet. Then later on, you decide to go with green instead of blue. Ordinarily, to make this change, you'd have to manually edit the color value at every place it appears in your stylesheet; however, Sass solves this problem by providing variables. You simply change the value of the variable and recompile the file, and the change will be reflected everywhere the variable was used. Here's an example Sass code snippet:

```
$primary-color: #00f; // first variable
$white: #fff; // second variable

.button{
  background: $primary-color; // first variable used
  color: $white; // second variabled used
}
```

Compiling this Sass code will generate the following output:

```
.button{
  background: #00f;
  color: #fff;
}
```

You can also create functions in Sass that help you separate repeatable CSS properties. Nested-rule capabilities are yet another advantage of using Sass. We'll cover some of these features as we proceed through the chapter. If you are keen to learn more about Sass, visit the official website.[1]

Customizing Foundation is very easy using Sass, as Foundation gives you access to the Sass variables and functions that were used to generate the default CSS file. For this we'll download the Sass version of Foundation, which contains all the Sass files used to generate the CSS file, as well as some other files that we'll cover very soon.

The best way to create a Sass version of a Foundation project is to use Foundation's command line interface, or CLI for short. It gives you the option to create new Foundation projects by writing a single command-line statement. If you're planning to use Foundation and customize it with Sass, we'd recommend that you download Foundation CLI, which we'll cover shortly.

If You Prefer Vanilla

We're going to be working with a number of different tools and using the command line in this chapter. Although we'll be providing step-by-step instructions, if you find it too tricky you can always stick with vanilla Foundation and use your **app.css** to customize the framework instead.

---

[1] http://sass-lang.com/

Installing Foundation CLI

We'll require some tools installed on our machines before we can install Foundation CLI:

- Git
- Node.js
- Ruby 1.9+

Here's some help should you need it.

Installing Git

The easiest way to install Git is to download the installer.[2] Click on the appropriate operating system and, once downloaded, double-click on it and follow the instructions.

To check if you have successfully installed Git, open a terminal (Terminal in OS X, Command Prompt in Windows) and type `git --version`. It should display the installed version of Git.

Installing Node.js

To install Node.js download its package from nodejs.org,[3] then double-click on the package and follow the instructions.

You can check if Node.js was installed successfully by typing `node -v` in your system terminal. It should display the currently installed version of Node.js.

Installing Ruby

If you're using a Macintosh machine, you'll probably have Ruby pre-installed. Go to the terminal and run the command `ruby -v`. It should display the version number of the currently installed version.

For different operating systems, appropriate Ruby installers can be found at https://www.ruby-lang.org/en/documentation/installation/#installers.

---

[2] http://git-scm.com/download

[3] https://nodejs.org

Installing Foundation CLI

To manage its own updates—as well as those for third-party libraries—Foundation uses Bower.[4] If you're unfamiliar with Bower, it's a client-side package manager that keeps track of packages that a developer uses. In this case, the package we need is the Foundation framework. We also require `grunt-cli`, a JavaScript program that runs various predefined tasks for Foundation CLI. You can read more about Grunt at http://gruntjs.com.

Open the terminal and type the following command:

```
npm install -g bower grunt-cli
```

Now let's install Foundation CLI using the following command:

```
gem install foundation
```

Permission Errors

If you run into any permission errors using these two commands, add the word `sudo` in front of them and enter your system password if prompted. This should fix your problem. If you experience other issues, we'd recommend you head over to the SitePoint Forums.[5]

After you're done executing the commands, type the following to check if Foundation was installed properly

```
foundation version
```

It should return a version number. In my case it returned `v1.0.4`, which means Foundation CLI v1.0.4 was installed on my system.

Now we're done installing the Foundation CLI. In the next section, we'll install a Sass compiler that will recompile the Sass file whenever we modify the Foundation's default Sass files.

---

[4] http://bower.io/

[5] http://community.sitepoint.com/

Installing Compass and Creating a Sass Foundation Project

Compass is an open-source CSS authoring framework that uses the Sass stylesheet language. It compiles Sass into static CSS stylesheets.

Installing Compass is extremely straightforward. You simply type the following command:

```
gem install compass
```

Once installed, navigate to a folder where you generally keep all your projects using the terminal; for example, `cd Documents`. Next, type the following command to generate your first Sass-compatible Foundation project:

```
foundation new First_project
```

This will create a new project called `First_project`. We'll cover every folder and file in this project in the section that follows.

There's another step to perform after creating a new Foundation project: running the `bundle` command. This command ensures that we're using the correct libraries mentioned in the **Gemfile** file that's present in the root folder. If you open this file, you'll see that it has the version of `sass` and `compass` included in it. The `bundle` command is very useful when you are changing the environment of the project, such as switching to a new system.

What's the Gemfile?

Gemfile keeps the list of gem dependencies of your Rails application. The dependencies are met by Bundler by running `bundle`.

You have to run this `bundle` command once for every new project. Install Bundler using this command:

```
gem install bundler
```

You can read more about bundler on its official website.[6]

Once bundler is installed, navigate to the newly created folder `/First-project` and run the `bundle` command as follows:

```
cd First_project
bundle
```

After the `bundle` command installs everything, run the following to make Compass watch for any changes that we make to our Sass files, and if any changes are made, compile them instantaneously:

```
bundle exec compass watch
```

Let's check to see if Compass is really working. Just to test it out, ppen the `sc-ss/app.scss` file and define a new Sass variable at the bottom:

```
$mycolor: #FFF;
```

Once the file is saved, you should see Compass executing some commands in the terminal:

```
modified scss/app.scss
write stylesheets/app.css
```

Make sure you delete the `$mycolor` variable that was defined previously and save the file again before closing it.

Understanding Foundation's Sass Project Structure

The contents of the `First_project` folder should look a little like Figure 7.1.

[6] http://bundler.io/

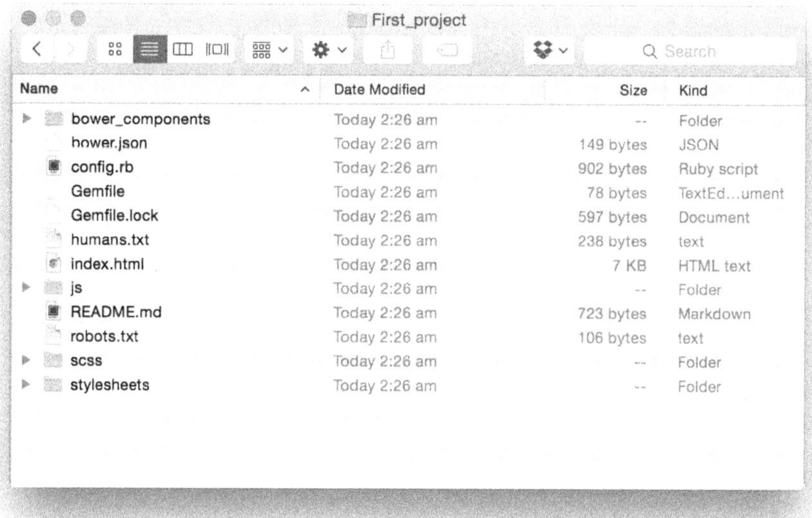

Figure 7.1. Foundation's Sass Project structure

It's time to understand some of the important files and folders inside this project. The first is the folder `bower_components`, with Bower managing its contents. It contains various third-party libraries such as **fastclick.js**, jQuery, Modernizr, and so on. It's recommended that you avoid changing anything inside this folder as it could result in conflicts.

bower.json is a manifest file that's used by Bower to keep track of the various third-party libraries used by a particular project. If you open this file, it should look similar to this:

bower.json

```
{
  "name": "foundation-compass-app",
  "version": "0.0.1",
  "private": "true",
  "dependencies": {
```

```
    "foundation": "zurb/bower-foundation"
  }
}
```

Suppose that you want to install AngularJS in this project. You can download it using a Bower command such as:

```
bower install angular --save
```

Bower will download the AngularJS package in the folder **bower_components/angular** and create a new entry in the **bower.json** file:

```
{
  "name": "foundation-compass-app",
  "version": "0.0.1",
  "private": "true",
  "dependencies": {
    "foundation": "zurb/bower-foundation",
    "angular": "~1.4.1"
  }
}
```

Bower is convenient because you can simply ignore the folder **bower_components** while sharing your project. Whoever you share the project with simply runs the following command, which promptly installs the dependencies:

```
bower install
```

This creates the **bower_components** folder for them, with all the required dependencies inside.

config.rb is a Compass configuration file that directs Compass where to look for appropriate files in the project. For example, it tells Compass where to locate the Sass files and where to store the static CSS files after compiling. If you open this file, it should look as follows:

```
add_import_path "bower_components/foundation/scss"
http_path = "/"
css_dir = "stylesheets"
```

```
sass_dir = "scss"
images_dir = "images"
javascripts_dir = "js"
```

The **scss** folder contains files for Foundation customization. It has two main files, namely: **_settings.scss** and **app.scss**. We will cover the details of these files in the next section.

The **stylesheet** folder contains all the static and compiled CSS files. By default, it has a file called **app.css** that has to be included in every HTML file of our web app. It's recommended to not make any changes to **app.css** file if you are customizing using Sass as they will be overridden when Compass recompiles Sass files.

Okay, now that we've installed everything we need and had a look at the directory structure, let's proceed to the fun part: looking at some Sass customization of Foundation.

Customizing Foundation Using Sass

In this section, we'll learn a bit about Sass and how to use it to customize Foundation's default styles. We'll cover the basics of Sass such as creating variables, nesting CSS, and functions. Covering the full details of Sass itself, however, is outside the scope of this book, but you can always refer to the official documentation[7] to dive deeper into Sass. You can also refer to the SitePoint tutorial "Getting Started with Sass"[8] and article "An Introduction to Sass in Rails"[9] for more Sass insights.

All Sass customizations to Foundation are done using two files present inside the **scss** folder: **_settings.scss** and **app.scss**. Let's see what each one does.

Working With _settings.scss

The first file **_settings.scss** contains commented variables for every predefined CSS and JavaScript component in Foundation. To customize a component, you just need to find a particular variable using **Ctrl + F** or **Cmd + F**, uncomment it, and then change the value in the file.

---

[7] http://sass-lang.com/documentation/file.SASS_REFERENCE.html

[8] http://www.sitepoint.com/getting-started-sass-bourbon/

[9] http://www.sitepoint.com/an-introduction-to-sass-in-rails/

Once you save the file, Compass will recompile the Sass and generate a new `app.css` file, which will go in the **stylesheet** folder.

Let's try out some Sass customization. Navigate to **First_project** and load the **index**.`html` file in your browser. You can see that there are many default Foundation components displayed in this file, as shown in Figure 7.2.

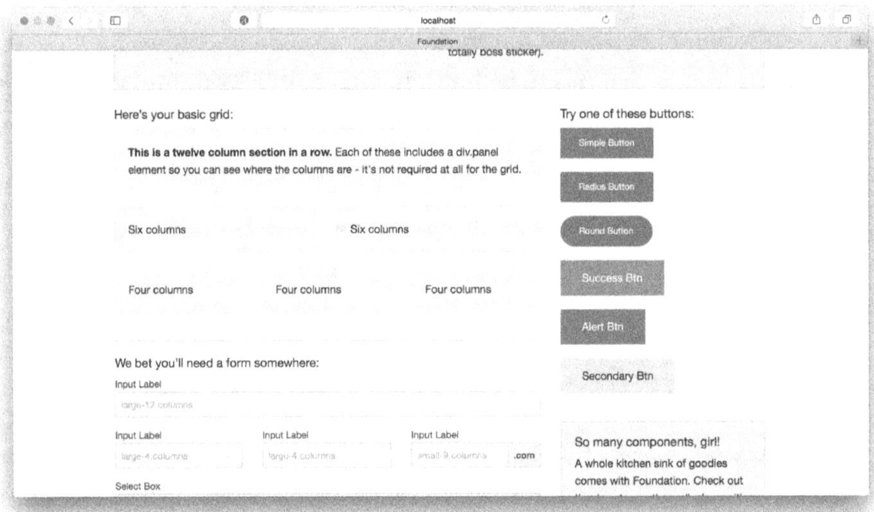

Figure 7.2. Example **index.html**

Let's make some modifications to the default button style . Open **_settings.scss** and search for `Buttons` in this file. You will come across a set of commented variables used for styling buttons, as seen in Figure 7.3.

```
// 05. Buttons
// - - - - - - - - - - - - - - - - - - - - - - - - -

// $include-html-button-classes: $include-html-classes;

// We use these to build padding for buttons.
// $button-tny: rem-calc(10);
// $button-sml: rem-calc(14);
// $button-med: rem-calc(16);
// $button-lrg: rem-calc(18);

// We use this to control the display property.
// $button-display: inline-block;
// $button-margin-bottom: rem-calc(20);

// We use these to control button text styles.
// $button-font-family: $body-font-family;
// $button-font-color: $white;
// $button-font-color-alt: $oil;
// $button-font-tny: rem-calc(11);
// $button-font-sml: rem-calc(13);
// $button-font-med: rem-calc(16);
// $button-font-lrg: rem-calc(20);
// $button-font-weight: $font-weight-normal;
// $button-font-align: center;

// We use these to control various hover effects.
// $button-function-factor: -20%;

// We use these to control button border styles.
```

Figure 7.3. Commented variables for styling buttons

Now uncomment the following line:

```
// $button-font-align: center;
```

And change it to:

```
$button-font-align: left;
```

Compass will override the default `text-align` property from the `button` class in **app.css**:

```
.button{
    ⋮
    text-align: left; //changed from center to left
    ⋮
}
```

Next, uncomment this line:

```
// $button-margin-bottom: rem-calc(20);
```

Changing it to:

```
$button-margin-bottom: rem-calc(40);
```

Compass will override the default `margin` property of the `button` class in **app.css**:

```
.button{
    ⋮
    margin: 0 0 2.5rem; // originally it was 0 0 1.5rem
    ⋮
}
```

Introducing rems

`Rem-calc` is a Foundation Sass function that converts pixel measurements to rems, so you can still think in pixels and end up with scalable ems. If you're unfamiliar with this new rem CSS unit, refer to the CSS-Tricks article "Confused about REM and EM?"[10].

We've already seen how to define a variable in Sass. You can use such variables to define a color scheme for your website. Let's create a new file that will store some re-useable colors for our website.

Create a new file **_colors.scss** inside the folder **sass** and add three new variables into it:

[10] https://css-tricks.com/confused-rem-em/

_colors.scss

```
$theme-primary-color: #009688;
$theme-secondary-color: #4DB6AC;
$theme-text-color: #212121;
```

Now, edit the file **app.scss**, which is inside the **sass** folder. We'll add the following code to the top of this file to include our newly created **colors.scss** file:

```
@import "colors";
```

What's with the underscores at the start of filenames?

Sass filenames that start with an underscore are called **partials**. This indicates that they are incomplete Sass files as they depend on other Sass files for variables and functions. If you remove the underscore from a filename, Compass will generate a new static CSS file of the same name.

Now that we have our theme colors defined, let's create a new class which, when attached to any paragraph element, will make it stand out from the rest. We'll use our theme colors in this class definition. Edit the **_settings.scss** file and add the following Sass code at the bottom of the file:

```
.standout-paragraph{
    color: $theme-text-color;
    padding: 20px;
    background-color: $theme-secondary-color;
}
```

Once compiled, the aforementioned code will have values such as:

```
.standout-paragraph{
    color: #212121;
    padding: 20px;
    background-color: #4DB6AC;
}
```

Nesting is a great way of organizing and maintaining CSS styles. Let's look at nesting in Sass by modifying the Sass code of `.standout-paragraph`:

```
.standout-paragraph{
    color: $theme-text-color;
    padding: 20px;
    background-color: $theme-secondary-color;
    //Nested Type 1
    a{
        color: #FFFFFF;
        text-decoration: none;
    }
    //Nested Type 2
    &.white-text{
        color: #FFFFFF;
    }
}
```

In this code, we have nested two new definitions: for `<a>` elements and for the `white-text` class. Let's check out the resulting output:

```
.standout-paragraph{
    color: #212121;
    padding: 20px;
    background-color: #4DB6AC;
}

//Nested type 1 results in the following
.standout-paragraph a{
    color: #FFFFFF;
}

//Nested type 2 results in the following
.standout-paragraph.white-test{
    color: #FFFFFF;
}
```

As seen in the CSS code, the nested type 1 results in CSS hierarchy that is `.standout-paragraph a`. However, nested type 2 is a way of referencing the parent selector with the help of the `&` symbol.

Hopefully this has given you a basic understanding of nesting in Sass. For further reading, refer to the Sass documentation's nesting section.[11]

[11] http://sass-lang.com/documentation/file.SASS_REFERENCE.html#nested_rules

Understanding app.scss

We'll move to the next important file in the **scss** folder, which is **app.scss**. This is the parent Sass file from which the main `app.css` file is created for the project, and is also where all the partial Sass files get imported. As mentioned above, partials are Sass files which cannot be compiled independently. They may have variables and functions that are defined in other Sass files.

If you open the **app.scss** file, it should have three import statements at the top:

```
@import "colors";
@import "settings";
@import "foundation";
```

The first two files are present in the **scss** folder; however, the last file, **foundation.scss**, is imported from the **/bower_components/foundation/scss/foundation.scss** location.

You will also find many commented import statements in this **app.scss** file, such as:

```
// @import
//   "foundation/components/accordion",
//   "foundation/components/alert-boxes",
//   "foundation/components/block-grid",
```

They are mainly provided so that you can select to include just the components that are required for your application. You can do so by commenting out the `@import "foundation";` line and uncommenting individual components from line five onwards.

For example, if you choose to skip the accordion, flex-video, and joyride components, you can uncomment the rest of the components and leave these components commented. To do so, you need to comment this line:

```
// @import "foundation";
```

And uncomment these lines as follows:

```
@import
  "foundation/components/accordion",
  "foundation/components/flex-video",
  "foundation/components/joyride";
```

The **app.scss** file is also the place to include new styles for your project. In the previous section, we had created a definition for `standout-paragraph` and its children elements inside the **_settings.scss** file. As **_settings.scss** file is imported at the top of **app.scss** file, there is the possibility of it being overridden by other imports below it. Hence, it is highly recommended that you write new Sass code at the end of the **app.scss** file.

Summary

In this chapter, we learned how to set up the Sass version of Foundation through Foundation CLI. We also covered how to install and set up Bower and Compass. Once Sass is set up, you can do so much more than mere customization. You can create new Sass partials and import them into **app.scss**, as well as add fresh classes and styles through new Sass files for your project.

And so we've reached the end of our journey exploring the Foundation framework, although I'd prefer to think of it as laying the foundations for future travels. I trust after this introduction that you're as excited as I am about the potential of the Foundation framework. If you're still keen to seek out more, you can also refer to the Foundation articles on SitePoint[12] to learn more about what you can do with the Foundation framework. Here are a few other useful links:

- Semantic Markup with Foundation 5 and Sass[13]
- Foundation 5 documentation[14]
- Example websites built using Foundation[15]
- Free Foundation templates[16]

---

[12] http://www.sitepoint.com/?s=foundation
[13] http://www.sitepoint.com/semantic-markup-foundation-5-sass/
[14] http://foundation.zurb.com/docs/
[15] http://foundation.zurb.com/learn/website-examples.html
[16] http://foundation.zurb.com/templates.html

- Foundation font icons[17]

I hope you enjoyed reading this book and trying out Foundation. Best of luck with your future web projects, and your journey with Foundation!

---

[17] http://zurb.com/playground/foundation-icon-fonts-3

www.ingramcontent.com/pod-product-compliance
Lightning Source LLC
LaVergne TN
LVHW080848170826
845678LV00006B/1743

* 9 7 8 0 9 9 2 4 6 1 2 7 0 *